100 Ideas for Secondary Teachers

Assessment for Learning

Bloomsbury Education
An imprint of Bloomsbury Publishing Plc

50 Bedford Square
London
WC1B 3DP
UK

1385 Broadway
New York
NY 10018
USA

www.bloomsbury.com

BLOOMSBURY and the Diana logo are trademarks of
Bloomsbury Publishing Plc

First published in 2015

ISBN
PB: 9781472911001
ePub: 9781472911025
ePDF: 9781472911018

4 6 8 10 9 7 5 3

Typeset by Newgen Knowledge Works (P) Ltd., Chennai, India
Printed and bound in Great Britain by CPI Group (UK) Ltd, Croydon CR0 4YY

100 Ideas for Secondary Teachers

Assessment for Learning

David Spendlove

BLOOMSBURY

LONDON • OXFORD • NEW YORK • NEW DELHI • SYDNEY

Other titles available in the 100 Ideas for Secondary Teachers series:

Everyone can learn but not always today and not always in your way!

This book is dedicated to all those inspirational teachers who simply don't give up on their pupils.

@david_spendlove
davidspendlove.wordpress.com

Online resources accompany this book at:
www.bloomsbury.com/100ideas-SecondaryAFL

Please type the URL into your web browser and follow the instructions to access the resources. If you experience any problems, please contact Bloomsbury at:
companionwebsite@bloomsbury.com.

Contents

Part 4: Increasing pupil ownership,
autonomy and success through AfL **83**

Introduction

Imagine that you went to your doctor, and they somehow, miraculously, told you what your condition was, but didn't tell you what medication or treatment you needed to get better. I would guess you would be confused, frustrated and slightly concerned as they shouted 'next patient!'. Well, the parallels with education are far too apparent, as this is the equivalent of assessment *of* learning, which has tended to dominate teaching in many schools. Pupils are told their summative 'learning condition' but are not told the formative information on how to 'get better'.

It is important to note that this book isn't an attack on the use of such summative and performance type assessments. However, what we do know is that if we want children to improve their 'learning condition' then the balance between 'assessment *of* learning' (summative) and 'assessment *for* learning' (formative) has to be correct, otherwise valuable learning opportunities and pupil gains are lost.

Assessment *for* learning (AfL) is therefore about better diagnostic assessment and formative teaching and learning; with learning being the central focus of teacher and pupil self-assessments (yes, pupils assessing themselves and others is essential). Such practices are still often misunderstood, even though the impact upon learners can be significant. All teachers should have access to a toolkit of AfL strategies to use in their lessons to ensure that all learners make rapid and sustained progress in their learning.

Unfortunately, AfL still remains a largely underdeveloped concept in many schools, yet it is one of the most powerful evidence-based approaches to improving teaching and learning. This book will provide AfL opportunities to be used in the context of the new Ofsted framework and new Teachers' Standards, and will explore practical 'toolkit' strategies for implementing AfL in everyday teaching.

Finally, AfL is not a fad or something trendy that will disappear. It is simply a way of capturing how learning is enhanced through diagnostic and dynamic assessments, with the associated two-way feedback processes being so focused and precise that they will ultimately increase the quality of teaching, learning, ownership, autonomy and confidence in the classroom.

How to use this book

This book includes quick, easy, practical ideas for you to dip in and out of, to support you in using assessment for learning strategies.

Each idea includes:

- A catchy title, easy to refer to and share with your colleagues.
- A quote from a teacher or student describing their experiences of the idea that follows or a problem they may have had that using the idea solves.
- A summary of the idea in bold, making it easy to flick through the book and identify an idea you want to use at a glance.
- A step-by-step guide to implementing the idea.

Each idea also includes one or more of the following:

Teaching tip

Some extra advice on how or how not to run the activity or put the strategy into practice.

Taking it further

Ideas and advice for how to extend the idea or develop it further.

Bonus idea ★

There are 18 bonus ideas in this book that are extra exciting and extra original.

Online resources also accompany this book. When the link to the resource is referenced in the book, log on to www.bloomsbury. com/100ideas-SecondaryAFL to find the extra resources, catalogued under the relevant idea number.

Share how you use these ideas in the classroom and find out what other teachers have done using **#100ideas.**

Questioning, thinking and dialogue

Part 1

Two million questions

"Judge a teacher by their questions, not their answers."

Questioning strategies often feel unnatural but they are central to promoting thinking in others.

Many research studies show that teachers ask lots of questions. Often a single lesson will include 50 to 60 questions, with a total of 300 to 350 being asked every day. Multiplying this by five days a week, the number of working days and an average length teaching career gives a very rough estimate of around two million questions per teacher. That's a lot of questions!

Questioning is something that many teachers struggle with, as it is counterintuitive – where else in life do you ask a question when you already know the answer? Here are five tips to improve your questioning:

- If a pupil gives a wrong answer, try probing for the correct answer.
- Make sure to identify those pupils who don't know the answer, rather than just taking answers from those who do know.
- Allow enough time for pupils to genuinely think about answers to a question (teachers often leave as little as a second for pupil thinking).
- Make sure that questions are sufficiently demanding.
- Involve as many pupils as possible in thinking about answers to a question (only about 25% of pupils are usually involved in classroom questioning).

Taking it further

Questioning is probably the most important tool in the teacher toolkit for developing and monitoring pupil learning. Use self-analysis, audio or video recording, or peer-observation to assess your questioning against the tips given here.

Fast and slow questions

"The brain is a wonderful organ. It starts working the moment you get up in the morning and does not stop until you get into school!"

Being aware of different types of questions will allow you to plan your questioning to achieve the greatest impact on learning.

It is generally regarded that we have two types of thinking. System one (fast) is survival thinking and system two (slow) is processed thinking.

In a classroom context, fast thinking questions will be those to which pupils already know the answer without having to think. Examples would be fast recall type questions such as names or dates – pupils either know the answer or they don't.

Slow thinking questions are those that require pupils to think and require much more processing to arrive at an answer. Examples would be questions that require pupils to analyse or evaluate in order to arrive at an answer.

When planning questions, make sure that you get a good balance of fast thinking and slow thinking questions in order to make sufficient demand upon pupils. Generally, slow thinking questions will make the greatest cognitive demand on pupils and are likely to lead to greater learning.

Pause, Pause, Share

"A simple reminder for AfL: Pupils should be working harder than the teacher."

The use of a 'wait time' or pause is generally understood as being beneficial to learning. Introducing a second wait or pause can also have a significant impact upon learning.

Research has shown that teachers typically leave little more than 1.5 seconds for pupils to respond to a question. We also know from research that the use of a 'wait time' after asking a question can increase the amount of thinking time and increase the level of participation of pupils.

Many teachers, however, often don't realise that a second wait time also increases the amount of thinking and participation. A simple way to remember this is Pause, Pause, Share or PPS:

- **P** – Teacher asks a question and pauses without giving or taking an answer.
- **P** – The teacher then signals they will take an answer from a targeted pupil, but instead of indicating if the answer is correct the teacher asks the group if the answer is correct, or if anyone can expand upon the answer. There then follows a second pause without taking the answer.
- **S** – The teacher then takes a final answer from a targeted pupil and shares and expands upon the answer with the group.

Teaching tip

Teachers often ask how long the pause should be when using wait times. The answer is that this will depend upon the question and the group you are teaching, so it is worth experimenting. Typically, teachers pause for less than a second of wait time, which is clearly insufficient. A pause time of three to five seconds would seem a sufficient amount of thinking time.

Taking it further

Teachers often find pausing before taking an answer or giving the answer quite difficult. Using a visual timer (for example a PowerPoint timer) so that pupils can see how long the pause will be can help overcome this difficulty.

Questioning repertoire

"Good teachers ask better questions and as a result get better answers!"

Would you ask pupils a question you didn't know the answer to? If your answer is no, you may be missing out on great opportunities for extending pupils' thinking.

Research has shown that teachers tend to give most attention to those pupils who appear to know the answers to the questions and secondly to those on the front row of desks in a classroom. Those on the periphery of the classroom – notably the back and corners – are those who get the least attention and are asked fewest questions. Simple adjustments to teaching can have significant effects on learning therefore, as well as varying the questions you ask, it is also important to vary who you ask.

- Alternate questions between boys and girls. Also consider how you respond to pupils of different genders; it has been shown that teachers tend to give fuller answers to girls than boys.
- Move questions around in a predetermined pattern, such as starting at the corners then working your way in.
- Use random name generators so that all pupils are likely to be asked a question or at least think they will be asked a question. It is also important to note that the question should be asked before the name is selected.
- Use a beanbag, ball or other appropriate object for the person answering the question to hold – this changes the point of attention and signifies clearly who is in the 'hot seat'.

- Actively seek out those that have not participated.
- Create a culture where pupils know that not answering is not a way of getting out of the task. Have a ritual that you adopt for a 'don't know' response, for example, phone a friend.
- Use the 'echo' strategy to help pupils construct their answers; when a pupil partially answers help them phrase a fuller and clearer response.
- Try to provoke thinking with unusual and difficult 'wicked' questions.
- Start with the answer and ask what the question is.

Bonus idea ★

Having a standing item on departmental agendas about 'improving questioning' is one way of committing to continuous improvement in this area.

Taking it further

Using peer-to-peer coaching is a great way of improving a teacher's questioning repertoire. Getting colleagues to observe each other allows teachers to get feedback on the different types and frequency of questions they use. For example, simply ask a colleague to observe a lesson and map out where in the classroom and to whom you most frequently ask questions. Alternatively, ask them to note the types of question you ask. Analysing the results allows you to adapt your repertoire.

Socrates was right

"Education is the kindling of a flame, not the filling of a vessel."
Socrates

Using Socratic questions is a way of increasing understanding and promoting thinking.

Use the question stems below as the basis for planned questions to help increase the level of thinking and reflection for pupils.

Questions that seek clarification:

- Can you explain that . . .?
- What do you mean by . . .?
- Can you give me an example of . . .?
- How does that help . . .?
- Does anyone have a question to ask . . .?

Questions that probe reason and evidence:

- Why do you think that . . .?
- How do we know that . . .?
- What are your reasons . . .?
- Do you have evidence . . .?
- Can you give me an example/counter example . . .?

Questions that explore alternative views:

- Can you put it another way . . .?
- Is there another point of view . . .?
- What if someone were to suggest that . . .?
- What would someone who disagreed with you say . . .?
- What is the difference between those views/ ideas . . .?

Questions that test implications and consequences:

- What follows (or what can we work out from) what you say . . .?
- Does it agree with what was said earlier . . .?
- What would be the consequences of that . . .?
- Is there a general rule for that . . .?
- How could you test to see if it were true . . .?

Questions about the question/discussion:

- Do you have a question about that . . .?
- What kind of question is it . . .?
- How does what was said/the question help us . . .?
- Where have we got to/who can summarise so far . . .?
- Are we any closer to answering the question/ problem . . .?

Bonus idea ★

Socratic thinking is a form of critical thinking. It is a way of interrogating our natural assumptions and finding out what we might truly understand and believe. Such an approach moves from surface learning to deep learning and can be quite challenging for pupils (and the teacher). Therefore it is essential to create the correct learning environment where it is deemed 'safe' to hold what might appear to be contradictory views. Equally, it is important to acknowledge that 'cognitive dissonance', the challenge of holding conflicting views, is a productive means to deeper understanding.

Hands down heads up

"Analysis has shown that approximately only 20% of classroom questions promote thinking and often only a small number of pupils will participate."

Using a 'hands down heads up' approach increases pupil thinking and participation.

One of the most common and successful strategies for AfL is to move away from the normal 'question and answer' routine, where the teacher asks a question and any pupil who knows the answer shoots their hand up immediately. This is unproductive, as it often means the same pupils are answering over and over again, whilst not allowing time for others to think about the answer. Quick responses suggest a low-level question, and teachers can be so eager to get the correct answer that they will move on even if the answer provided isn't quite right.

To use a 'hands down heads up' strategy, inform the class that the question you are about to ask requires thinking about and will require everyone to have an answer (not just the usual suspects). After asking the question, give a sufficient wait time to allow everyone to think through his or her answer. Then use a random name or targeted name strategy to choose who you want to answer the question.

Whilst 'hands down heads up' is an incredibly simple strategy it is fundamental to increasing the amount of thinking taking place within a lesson.

Think – Pair – Share

"Two heads are better than one even when they are disagreeing."

It is unproductive to rely only on yourself as the sole source of encouraging learning in the classroom. Pairing pupils up is a powerful way to involve everyone in supporting learning.

In the traditional classroom the teacher has conventionally engaged with one pupil at a time whilst the rest of the group give the impression of being engaged – or sometimes don't pretend at all!

The simple strategy of 'Think – Pair – Share' engages the whole class in thinking, speaking and listening by getting pupils to share and clarify their thinking with partners. Start by asking a big question, followed by 'wait time', allowing individuals to consider their own response. Then ask pupils to discuss the question with a partner to arrive at a joint response. This releases the teacher to be more effective through planned strategic intervention with small groups, rather than reacting to dominant individuals. Finally, take joint response answers from the pairs as desired.

Central to this idea is the concept of PIES. See Idea 77 for more details.

Teaching tip

Give careful thought to the dynamics of the pairings. Mixing the pairings in terms of ability and gender can provide additional benefits.

Dialogic talk and questioning

"Dialogic teaching harnesses the power of talk to stimulate and extend students' thinking." Robin Alexander

Central to AfL are classroom discussions to increase the amount of thinking and reflection amongst pupils.

Teaching tip

Good dialogic questions start with 'Why do you think . . . ?', 'How do you know . . . ?', 'Why might this be true/untrue?'

Dialogic talk and questioning is based around extended discussions and deeper thinking. However, simply having a long answer is not enough – more important is the thinking behind it. Central features of dialogic talk and questioning are:

- The teacher's questions are structured to provoke thoughtful answers and reflection. Pupil's answers provoke further questions and dialogue with each other.
- Learners are encouraged to ask questions and provide explanations for each other.
- The teacher uses one-to-one monitoring with pupils, which is long enough to make a difference. The dialogue is formative rather than supervisory and provides clear feedback on which the learner can build.
- The learners who are not engaged in speaking actively participate through active listening, looking, reflecting and evaluating.
- The learning environment is designed to encourage participation and dialogic teaching and learning.
- A reciprocal environment is encouraged where teachers and learners listen to each other, share ideas and consider alternative viewpoints.
- The emotional environment is important and learners have the confidence to take risks, make mistakes, and deal with uncertainty.
- Questioning builds upon prior knowledge and elicits evidence of learner's understanding.

Target practice

"The important thing is not to stop questioning." Albert Einstein

There are many different types of targeted interventions that teachers can use to ensure they are providing effective, planned teaching and learning.

There is a familiar scenario in many classrooms where the teacher is really enjoying the lesson but only two or three pupils are actively engaged. The most effective way to overcome this is through planned 'targeted' interventions, where the teacher deliberately plans one-to-one interventions such as:

- Individual targeted questions in a group question and answer session.
- Targeted planned questions in a one-to-one session.
- A discussion relating to target setting.
- A discussion relating to misconceptions diagnosed as part of teacher assessment.
- A one-to-one discussion to identify a source of difficulty.
- An opportunity for the learner to feedback their progress related to their targets.
- An opportunity for pupils to co-construct and negotiate their next steps in learning.
- Feedback that focuses on individual improvement and progress.
- Bringing the learner into the assessment process (for example, understanding using assessment criteria).

Although unscheduled interventions should and will always take place, there should also be planned opportunities for targeted questions, quality diagnosis and feedback to ensure all learners are regularly and individually monitored.

Teaching tip

Targeted intervention is about the teacher and pupil gathering information in order to achieve the same learning goal. It is important to keep a log of the different types of targeted interventions that you use for each pupil.

Wicked questions

"Learning is better when it matters."

'Wicked questions' are questions with no obvious answer designed to probe thinking and understanding.

There are some forms of questions that you should try to avoid. Most notable are vague questions that no one really understands and pupils merely guess what might be in the teacher's head. There is a difference between these questions and questions deliberately designed to provoke thinking whilst demonstrating evidence of learning and deeper understanding – sometimes known as wicked questions. Wicked questions are:

- used to challenge assumptions that may not be sustainable
- questions where there is more than one answer
- questions that deliberately provoke or divide opinion
- questions that may present a paradox.

Example wicked questions include:

- Is there more love than hate in the world?
- Is it okay to bully a bully?
- If your brain were to be put into another person's skull and their brain put into your skull – which person would you be?
- Does charity simply increase the need for charities?

Obviously the nature of the questions can be changed depending on the age and subject being taught. However, the emphasis is on thinking through questions and developing and defending a position on a topic.

Question plans

"I found myself using questions to fill time and asking questions which required little thought from the students."

A lesson built around a collection of pre-planned questions can be used as an alternative to a normal lesson plan.

Questions are central to improved teaching using AfL. Not just any old questions but really good questions.

Very few teachers enter the classroom with pre-planned questions, and questioning can sink to low-level mundane and repetitive questions as a result. When analysed, only around 20% of questions actually require any real thinking from learners.

With AfL the status of question is elevated to a much more significant level by getting teachers to think about questions as the cornerstones of the learning experience.

Pre-plan your questions, and target them to specific groups of learners to be most effective. An often-quoted example of good practice is that of Japanese teacher question planning, where groups of colleagues plan questions together. The *jugyou kenkyuu* or 'lesson study' allows teachers to pre-plan and discuss deep probing questions designed to enhance learning. Central to this concept is that assessment is built in to the process of learning and not at the end.

Using 'question plans' as opposed to a 'lesson plan' to structure a lesson prioritises the learning above the functional aspects of planning and ensures learning is prioritised by remaining the key focus.

Teaching tip

Bear in mind the Ofsted criteria: 'teachers use questioning and discussion to assess the effectiveness of their teaching and promote pupils' learning'.

Taking it further

Sharing planned questions with pupils can be used as an alternative to sharing objectives. For example, explain that 'these are the questions that you can't answer at the start of the lesson but you will be able to answer at the end of the lesson'.

High-level questions

"Education is more than filling a child with facts. It starts with posing questions." D. T. Max

Shifting from low-level to high-level questions increases the challenge you place upon pupils. This process can be difficult and needs some planning.

There is a very funny Peter Kay sketch about the questions teachers ask, such as 'Do you know who I am?', 'How old are you?', 'Where should you be?', 'Who do you think you are?' Whilst the comedic delivery makes the lines above much funnier than they appear, it does illustrate how easy it is for the teacher to ask low-level questions in the classroom.

Combine the ideas High-level questions with Target practice, use of Pause, pause, share, Hands down heads up and Think – Pair – Share to develop a very sophisticated questioning repertoire (Ideas 12, 9, 3, 6, and 7 respectively).

Typical question stems for planning high-level questioning include:

Analysis (Examine relevant information to select best course of action)
What are other possible outcomes?
How is . . . similar to . . .?
What are some of the problems of . . .?
Can you distinguish between . . .?
What were some of the motives behind . . .?
What might someone else think differently about . . .?

Synthesis (Obtain evidence and expert opinion to aid decision-making)
Can you see a possible solution to . . .?
If you had access to all resources how would you deal with . . .?
What would happen if . . .?
How many ways can you . . .?
Can you create new and unusual uses for . . .?
Can you develop a proposal which would . . .?

Evaluation (Judge the value of something based upon considered personal values/opinions)
Is there a better solution to . . .?
How could X be considered better than Y?
Can you defend your position about . . .?
Do you think . . . is a good or a bad thing?
How would you have handled . . .?
What changes to . . . would you recommend?

Metacognition 1

"Metacognition can be defined as thinking about thinking."

Metacognition is regarded as one of the most powerful ways of improving learner's outcomes as the process encourages thinking about our own thinking in a meaningful way.

When employing metacognition, instead of coming up with an answer to a question, we think about how we came up with the answer and interrogate the rules we used to get an answer. As such, metacognition is explicitly linked to AfL as it encourages deep and meaningful understanding and autonomy.

There are two clear aspects to consider:

First, reflection upon thinking, which means thinking about **what** we know. Encourage metacognition through questions such as:

- How does what you are doing help you?
- What one thing will you remember long after this lesson and why?
- What single question are you still trying to understand and why might this be?

Second, self-regulation in managing **how** we learn. Develop this area by asking pupils:

- to select a particular strategy for working through a problem
- to use peer review to decide how best to improve their work
- to predict the outcomes of different ways of working and which will result in the best progress
- to discuss the criteria by which the success of an activity is judged.

Teaching tip

Tell pupils about metacognition and what it means. Model the processes in your own work so that they can see metacognition in action.

Metacognition 2

"Having a metacognitive awareness means an individual not only has knowledge about themselves but it also includes knowledge about the strategies used to tackle problems." R. Fisher

Increasing pupils' thinking linked to AfL can have a significant impact upon learner outcomes.

Learning is impossible to see; we have to rely on proxies to indicate it is happening. Equally, we can't stop learning happening and we can't always control what is and isn't being learnt. Metacognitive activities provide opportunities to reflect on how we might learn, what we might be learning and how effective that learning may be.

Use planned questions to promote such thinking related to metacognition, such as:

- How did you come to that conclusion?
- Are there any other ways of thinking about this problem?
- What strategies are appropriate for solving this problem and why?
- What might other people's perspectives be on this?
- What strategies might you use to extract the additional information you need?
- How well are the different strategies working?
- How do you know you have got the right answer?
- How could this be interpreted in a different way?
- What do you need to know to be able to answer this better?
- How did you feel when you tried to answer the question?

Taking it further

Asking pupils to 'mind map' is an interesting way of getting them to show both what and how they are thinking about a topic. This allows you to ask how might they think about it differently.

Beyond Bloom

"What any person in the world can learn, almost all persons can learn if provided with appropriate prior and current conditions of learning." Benjamin Bloom

Recognising that learning can take place at different levels and in different ways and planning accordingly represents very powerful teaching.

Bloom's taxonomy is a simple way of thinking about the different levels of challenge that teachers create in their classroom, through the planning of both questions and learning objectives. Very briefly, Bloom's identified different levels of cognitive challenge ranging from low to high: *Knowledge, Comprehension, Application, Analysis, Synthesis,* and *Evaluation.*

An updated version, Anderson's taxonomy (below), identifies knowledge as factual, conceptual, procedural or metacognitive. This allows us to think about whether the challenges in a lesson such as the learning objectives or the questions being asked are sufficiently demanding.

To use the table, select one of the four types of knowledge (from low to high) and then select the level of cognitive demand. Where the noun of knowledge and the verb of the cognitive domain intersect is where the level of demand is characterised and built around, for example, 'Can you *conclude* from your experiment what the key changes were?'

Teaching tip

Bloom's taxonomy is significant as it shifted 1950s thinking away from teaching and more towards learning. Whilst different versions of Bloom's taxonomy exist the key principle of increasing cognitive load remains.

Cognitive Demand

Knowledge		Remember	Understand	Apply	Analyse	Evaluate	Create
	Factual	List	Summarise	Classify	Order	Rank	Combine
	Conceptual	Describe	Interpret	Experiment	Explain	Assess	Plan
	Procedural	Tabulate	Predict	Calculate	Differentiate	Conclude	Compose
	Metacognitive	Appropriate use	Execute	Construct	Achieve	Action	Actualise

Using feedback to ensure progress

Part 2

How cost effective is feedback?

"If you think education is expensive, try ignorance." Derek Bok

Evidence-based education increasingly tries to match research findings to practice. Nevertheless, it needs to be remembered that practice is highly dependent on the context it operates in and not all research is transferable.

What is the value (compared to cost) of one day's teaching – in terms of the payback to a society? Or if we want to be really inquisitive, what is the value of one lesson? Why would we want to know? Well, in a period of austerity providing just one extra hour of teaching to every pupil costs a significant sum of money; if there is no payback then why provide it?

In broad terms, research has shown that increasing the amount of teaching time outweighs the cost of providing that instruction and that increased grade performance does lead to increased labour market earnings. Nonetheless, if the teaching is not effective then there are no gains.

The next question, then, is about individual teacher effectiveness. It is regarded that effective teachers make an impact of around 40% difference upon student attainment. In relation to the payback from AfL, the Sutton Trust have created an Educational Endowment Foundation toolkit that highlights which educational interventions impact the most upon learning and identifies the associated costs.

A table showing those areas most related to AfL is available in the online resources.

Taking it further

As can be seen AfL related activities have high impact, low cost and are based upon generally good evidence. To find out more, visit educationendowment foundation.org.uk/toolkit/feedback

What does learning look like?

"Pupils' strengths and misconceptions are identified and acted on by teachers during lessons and . . . to plan future lessons." Ofsted school inspection handbook

Teachers often receive feedback on their teaching based upon what others believe learning to be. However, learning is not always as clear as it may seem.

There is a general misunderstanding about learning, because we can't actually see learning and, although we can see the outcomes of learning, we don't always know how the learning came about.

Whether you are an advocate of behaviourist (Skinner, etc.), cognitivist (Piaget, etc.) or constructivist (Vygotsky, etc.) approaches to learning, we all tend to equate certain characteristics as being indicators of learning:

- Pupils are busy.
- Pupils are responding, engaged and motivated.
- The classroom is quiet and behaviour is good.
- Pupils seem to know what they are doing.
- The teacher is busy and working hard.

Unfortunately, these are only proxies of learning, but they have come to be viewed as indicators and measures of learning. It should be noted that such characteristics are not necessarily bad, but they are not true indicators of learning. Equally, we can't stop learning taking place. Children are learning all the time both, subconsciously and consciously, and often they are learning what we don't wish them to learn. Therefore the challenge of AfL is to ensure that more planned (than unplanned) and intended learning takes place.

Teaching tip

AfL can be more effective where there is a shared understanding and definition amongst teachers and learners of what learning is and the conditions in which learning is best developed.

Taking it further

Sharing good practice related to learning is important and should be encouraged through meetings, learning walks, teachmeets and newsletters.

Progress in lessons

"Research shows that although teachers often share learning intentions or objectives they still tend to reward and value neatness, quantity and notional effort!"

Many of the principles of AfL are central to ensuring progress in lessons is maintained.

Even though learners will naturally progress over time, it is important that teachers know how learners are progressing and that they are progressing in the right direction. However, pupils don't all progress at the same time in the same way in a linear manner – progress can be messy! When looking at single episodes of teaching and learning, progress really needs to be viewed by considering the learner's needs and the context in which the learning is taking place. Importantly, over time, the expectation is that a learner will not be in deficit in their understanding and that progress in a skill, concept or knowledge will grow over time. Monitor learning in the following ways:

- Differentiating the learning for various groups of learners.
- Engaging, challenging and motivating students in different ways.
- Using effective questioning to identify the different levels of understanding.
- Pupils engaged in self- and peer-assessment to monitor their own progress.
- A range of strategies is employed to gain feedback on pupil progress within the lesson.
- Feedback is used to inform both the direction of the lesson and planning for future lessons.
- Pupils have a shared understanding of what quality means and know how their performance is assessed.
- Pupils succeed in meeting the objectives for the lesson or episodes within the lesson.

Not all feedback is good feedback

"Feedback can be considered as 'reducing the discrepancy between current and desired understanding'." John Hattie and Helen Timperley

Feedback studies tend to report on all types of feedback. It is important that teachers reflect on what works for them in their environment.

In many research studies, feedback is overwhelmingly seen as one of the most important factors for improving learning, but some aspects of feedback are more important than others. The feedback areas with the greatest impact are, as you would expect, related to specific tasks and how to improve them.

Here are some tips to make your feedback more effective.

- Make sure it is not too frequent, as this may increase dependency on the teacher.
- Make it simple enough for a pupil to understand.
- Don't use feedback merely to reinforce something that the pupil knows is wrong.
- Use appropriate language.
- Make sure that any action required is within the control of the learner.
- Base feedback on intrinsic motivation rather than extrinsic rewards.
- Focus on where the learner is going, not where they are now.
- Don't use summative codes that have little meaning.
- Provide feedback at an appropriate time in the learning sequence.

Teaching tip

The more we explore feedback the more we realise how complex a topic it is. Be aware that it is almost impossible to stop giving feedback as it is communicated almost all of the time through non-verbal cues such as a smile, a subtle head movement, a hand signal and so on.

Taking it further

Every classroom and every pupil is different, so it is really important to find out what works for you in your environment, with your subject and pupils. Improve the impact of your feedback by investing time in finding out which feedback works best for you and your pupils.

Effective feedback

"Assessment is the means used by good teachers to evaluate that progress is being made and diagnose the needs of the pupil."

Not all feedback is effective; a simple checklist can help examine if you are getting it right.

Not all feedback is as productive as it might be. This simple checklist will help you identify if your feedback is heading in the right direction. It is also available to print as a questionnaire in the online resources.

- Is feedback clearly linked to the planned learning intentions?
- Do learners understand what quality means, in terms of the objective against which they are being assessed or are self-assessing?
- Do learners know the steps to progression and success, and is it clear what these mean?
- Does feedback present future targets which are clear, specific and achievable?
- Is feedback aimed at motivating the learner intrinsically?
- Is feedback clear and does it provide a clear way to improve on the original task?
- Does feedback contain written confirmation and guidance rather than a grade or mark?
- Is feedback phrased so it is not damaging to the pupil's self-esteem? (It has been found that computer feedback can be more productive than teacher feedback).
- Is feedback adjusted to take account of the learner, the context and stage of learning?
- Is feedback provided in different ways, for example, verbal, written, peer?

Feedback on the task or the learner?

"Assessment . . . should be the servant, not the master, of the curriculum." Department of Education and Science and the Welsh Office

Feedback can relate to both the learner and the task, but it has to be the right kind of feedback to be productive.

There is something of a dichotomy between whether feedback should be only on the task that is being completed or whether it should be on the learner, or both. In reality, it depends on the situation, context and nature of the feedback.

Research shows that if you are going to feedback on a person's disposition then focusing on their effort (for example, perseverance on a task) will have greater impact than focusing on their perceived innate ability, such as intelligence.

Carol Dweck noted research where 11 year olds were given a series of simple puzzles, with each student given a score plus six words of feedback. Half of the group were praised for intelligence and half praised for their effort. The students were then given a choice of an easy or difficult test to take.

Only one third of those who received feedback on their innate ability chose the harder test, and overall they showed a 20% decrease in their performance. Meanwhile, 90% of those who received feedback on their effort chose the harder test, and this group showed a 30% increase in performance.

Therefore, to make the most of feedback, focus it on the objectives of the task and the dispositions of the individual in relation to the effort they applied to the task.

Teaching tip

It has been shown that teachers can tend to reward perceived effort rather than capability in completing a task. As such there is often an unproductive mismatch between the task and the feedback, which will have little impact on the learner. A way of overcoming this is the use of teacher 'blind' marking (where the names of the pupils are removed from the work) or through peer blind marking where pupils mark others' work without knowing who the work belongs to.

Faults and fixes

"Focusing on improving feedback will have an almost immediate positive effect."

It is important to have the correct classroom environment for peer-to-peer work to be successful. This means that there should be a shared understanding of the benefits of carrying out peer-to-peer work.

Using a 'faults and fixes' table (see the example below) provides an easy way to structure a peer review exercise. When using the table pupils will be peer-assessing each other's work against set criteria, which has been established and shared.

Introduce the table by saying 'you now have five minutes to review your partner's work and complete the table by identifying five faults and recommending five fixes'.

Fault	Fix
1.	1.
2.	2.
3.	3.
4.	4.
5.	5.

Feedback without grading

"What is surprising is that giving marks and comments together produces no improvement." Dylan Wiliam and Paul Black

Providing feedback and a grade at the same time can cancel out some of the benefits of formative feedback

One of the most significant elements to come out of the AfL research is that feedback that has detailed and specific information, that focuses the learner's attention on what needs to be addressed in relation to their work, is the most advantageous.

Evaluative feedback, such as a mark or grade, may be helpful in telling you where you are as a learner but it doesn't tell you how to improve. Such summative grades can be useful for the teacher in terms of data analysis, but when grades and a comment are used at the same time it appears that the effect of the feedback is decreased.

Research by Lipnevich suggests this is because it reduces a 'sense of self-efficacy and elicits negative affect around the assessment task'. Therefore the mark acts as a distraction from engaging with the feedback.

Providing high-quality feedback has a more profound effect than grading, so think hard about what is more appropriate when marking a task.

Teaching tip

Bear in mind the Ofsted criteria requirement: 'Teachers systematically and effectively check pupils' understanding throughout lessons, anticipating where they may need to intervene and doing so with notable impact on the quality of learning.'

Marking as a two-way process

"Formative assessment is not a test but a process that produces not so much a score but a qualitative insight into student understanding." W. James Popham

Often marking is seen as a one-way street. However, having a dialogue with pupils via marking creates a two-way process.

Often when a teacher marks books it is a one-way process: the teacher collects the books, adds some comments, hands the books back and hopes that the pupil reads the comments.

Turning this into a two-way process makes marking a much more productive activity. Instead of simply adding comments, a more effective way of encouraging dialogue is to ask questions in the marking feedback. Example questions are 'How do you know?', 'Can you explain how you decided this?' or 'Why might this be incorrect?' Such questions deliberately try to provoke thinking and dialogue rather than the teacher simply doing the thinking for the pupil by marking something as correct.

For this to be effective, time has to be made available for learners to respond to the questions.

Angry Birds

"Any assessment that helps a pupil to learn and develop is formative." Phillippe Perrenoud

Certain types and timing of feedback better lend themselves to different activities.

One good example of this is the type of feedback used in games. Apologies if you have never come across 'Angry Birds', which is a very popular game played by millions of people on smartphones and tablets. There are interesting similarities between this type of game and AfL principles:

- The task is very clear.
- The criteria for success are clear.
- Progression through meeting the criteria is well defined.
- Feedback is rapid.
- Support from others is encouraged.
- Creative risks are encouraged.
- Self-evaluation is built in.

Although Angry Birds is a game, it highlights how pupils learn autonomously and intuitively when they wish to. It also illustrates that the key principles of AfL are evident in pupils' day to day experiences and that they can be a powerful motivator. Failure at a task is not seen as the end of an experience but as feedback to improve performance by building upon prior experiences. Therefore the feedback is seen as a positive motivator rather than de-motivator. It is important to note that this type of feedback is most powerful when it is matched to the correct activity.

Accept or amend

"You either accept or amend the comments – you decide!"

Central to any peer review process is collating the different views of those involved in the review process.

Using the 'accept or amend' template (the template is available in the online resources) provides a really useful structure for carrying out peer review using Post-it notes.

First, assign each pupil at least three pieces of work to peer review, making notes on a Post-it, so that each pupil has their work reviewed by at least three peers.

The completed notes are then pasted on the sheet. The pupil whose work has been reviewed has to consider their response to the three comments and indicate whether they accept the comments or whether they feel they need amending.

For example, a pupil may accept the comments and then go and make the suggested improvements to their work. However, a pupil may also choose to amend the comments. This could be where they feel they haven't been correctly assessed against the criteria or where the person assessing has interpreted their work incorrectly.

The teacher's role in this process also changes as they comment only on the accept or amend sheet (not the actual work), feeding back and moderating the comments, and indicating whether the comments were fair or whether the adjustment was necessary. This means the teacher is honing the learners' reflective skills rather than focusing purely on the work.

Regular plenaries

"It is important for students 'to hold a concept of quality roughly similar to that held by the teacher'." D. R. Sadler

Plenaries are a useful opportunity for gaining feedback, but it is a misconception that they should only happen at the end of a lesson.

There is often a misconception that a plenary is something that only happens at the end of the lesson, and that it entails getting some form of feedback. For example, it is not uncommon to see teachers get pupils to review whether they have met the objectives of the lesson using a thumbs up, thumbs down approach. Whilst this has some virtues, it is often too late in the lesson. Therefore an alternative to the end-of-lesson plenary are lots of mini plenaries throughout the lesson to enable you:

- to check on progress made so far
- to gain feedback on a specific objective
- to find out what learning has taken place
- to identify individuals who need support or need challenging
- to summarise the key points so far
- to ask targeted questions
- to share and model emerging good practice
- to evaluate your teaching up to that point
- to challenge and adapt emerging poor practice
- to reorientate and refocus the learning
- to adjust your teaching according to the feedback
- to identify the next sequence of learning
- to identify the 'bonus objective'
- to praise
- to all take a breather – particularly if it is a long lesson!

Teaching tip

Plenaries are a good way to 'chunk up' the lesson into manageable teaching and learning parts. The length will be dependent on the age and concentration spans of pupils. For example, regular 10 or 15 minute chunks and plenaries may be appropriate for younger learners whilst older pupils may benefit from longer 20 to 30 minutes chunks.

Read, Reflect, Respond

"It is easier to build strong children than to repair broken men."
Frederick Douglass

Comment-only marking is seen as effective feedback, but this needs a structure such as Read, Reflect and Respond in order to increase the effectiveness.

One of the central features of AfL is moving towards comment-only marking as a means to increasing learning gains; this can be written or verbal comments. In the research into AfL learners were split into three groups:

- One group received marks only (for example, 7 out of 10).
- One group received comments only.
- One group received a combination of marks and comments.

It was found that the group who received comments only were the group that demonstrated the greatest learning gains.

Recognise that the quality of comments are critical, as the feedback needs to be specific, formative and related to the criteria for the task. Brief comments, or providing insufficient time, may have little impact. When using comment-only approaches the three R's should be followed:

- Read: pupils are given time to read comments – preferably at the start of the lesson.
- Reflect: pupils need to consider what the comments mean – this may involve a discussion with the teacher or another pupil.
- Respond: pupils then need to respond by putting into action the feedback they have received.

Instant 'live' feedback

"Technology is just a tool. In terms of getting the kids working together and motivating them, the teacher is the most important."
Bill Gates

New technology offers new ways of providing instant feedback remotely. Shared online documents allow collaborative work to take place in different ways.

New ways of working are emerging which allow teachers and pupils to work in real time having the equivalent of a sustained conversation about their work. There is one immediate danger with this: if you're not careful your whole life inside and out of school can be consumed with marking and feedback. Nonetheless, if managed effectively and with specific groups then this can give a greater gain with no extra effort.

Try using shared documents in online tools such as Google Docs, which allows the teacher to work both inside and outside the classroom on a live document that the pupil is working on – either as the work is in progress or once the document is in a finished state. This means that the work doesn't sit in a redundant pile on the teacher's desk but receives feedback when it most effective.

Target students and add feedback to the documents by selecting the comments function in Google Docs, and pupils will get instant live feedback even if they are not in the classroom. This means that by the time the final work is submitted the feedback has already been given in a timely manner, and the pupil has had time to act upon the advice.

Teaching tip

Using free online software, such as Google Docs, for spreadsheets, word processing and presentations means that teachers don't have to be concerned about pupil access or compatibility issues when working on assignments out of school. Once pupils have an account, which can be arranged via the school, teachers and pupils can collaborate on shared documents both in the creation and assessment of assignments.

Bonus idea ★

Using collaborative online software allows pupils to 'buddy edit' each others work as a form of peer-assessment. Pupils can be buddied up and given shared access to each others work to enable them to peer-assess online.

Visualisers

"The only good feedback is feedback which is acted upon."

Visually sharing high-quality work and exemplifying how it has been assessed gives pupils access to the mysterious world of assessment.

Teaching tip

If you don't have a visualiser you can simply scan a piece of work and then display it on the board with a projector. Alternatively, webcams can be used to display exercise books etc.

One of the central ingredients of AfL is that pupils understand explicitly how they are assessed and what 'quality' looks like so that they can become self-sufficient and are able to self-assess. For many pupils, however, how they are assessed remains a mysterious process and is something that is done to them, not for them.

An effective way of overcoming this is to engage pupils in a discussion about how a piece of work is about to be assessed or has been assessed, and a useful tool for this is a digital visualiser (sometimes called a document camera). If you haven't seen one of these devices, it is a relatively low cost web camera, which allows hard copy documents (for example, a pupil's exercise book) to be displayed on screen through a data projector.

Taking it further

Build in regular opportunities for self- and peer-assessment through using a visualiser so that it becomes part of a normal routine where pupils expect to share their work with others and self-assess their work as part of a group activity.

This allows a discussion to be had about how the work has been assessed and how it can be improved by working on the real document. If this is combined with an interactive whiteboard then the exercise can be enhanced by asking pupils to come to the interactive board and highlight certain features, for example, 'show me a place in the text where a comma is missing' or 'underline the most important sentence'. This means pupils gain an insight into the assessment process in a visual and interactive way.

Twitter feedback

"It is unlikely you know anyone who entered the teaching profession simply because they were good at assessing – yet it is a fundamental part of teaching!"

Twitter allows quick feedback of learning and encourages high-level thinking through synthesising key ideas.

Social networking has revolutionised learning and communication, but many schools have failed to fully recognise or capitalise on the powerful learning that social networks offer. It is nevertheless recognised that social networks do create problems, so often teachers will need to find ways around working within any constraints a school may have in place.

One of the biggest social networks is Twitter, which as a concept shouldn't really work. The concept of 'tweeting' a message of 140 characters makes little or no sense, yet there are around a billion tweets every week and many children use Twitter naturally as part of their everyday communication network.

What makes Twitter so powerful in AfL is the need for high-level thinking when synthesising a message into only 140 characters. Getting pupils to tweet their feedback at the end of the lesson, summarising a difficult concept or tweeting to a peer as part of peer-assessment, provides powerful learning and feedback scenarios.

If you are not allowed social media in the classroom, use a simple Twitter-style template (see the example available in the online resources) to encourage synthesising ideas via tweets.

Taking it further

Use a hashtag for a particular lesson, for example, #biology9.30myschool, to allow feedback to be both immediate and collated (but public!).

Bonus idea ★

There are a variety of Twitter voting systems available that you can use to conduct live polls during the lesson. For example, you can ask a question and when pupils answer you can see the results live on screen and therefore get instantaneous feedback.

Thirty seconds of digging

"Teaching takes place in time, but learning takes place over time."
P. Griffin

Encouraging self-diagnosis and providing time for self-reflection is a useful strategy for getting valuable feedback.

Imagine a doctor with 30 patients who all need treatment at the same time, and all with different symptoms, and you have something very similar to your average classroom.

So how do you capture the various learning conditions of your pupils?

One key way is through pupil self-diagnosis. Give learners 30 seconds (or more) of 'digging' time to unearth what they are struggling with. This could be a key concept, a learning objective, an aspect of an examination, etc. The point is to set aside time for self-diagnosis and that self-diagnosis is encouraged and practiced.

Collect feedback in a variety of ways, through Post-it notes, mini whiteboards, or pupil verbal feedback. The point is to get quick feedback from all pupils.

Synthesize and act upon the information. This could be by asking pupils to place their Post-it notes into different categories on a wall or by rearranging pupils into groups on the basis of the feedback received.

Digging encourages pupil self-diagnosis and reflection, it allows quick analysis, and most importantly it allows the teacher to gather such information quickly and then adjust the teaching situation.

Taking it further

Create a 'digging area' – a dedicated place or space where pupils instinctively share what they are struggling with, for example, a wall where Post-it notes can be posted throughout the lesson.

On your way out

"Rising familiarity with a text and fluency in reading it can create an illusion of mastery." Peter Brown

Using Post-it notes to gain feedback as pupils leave a lesson is an excellent way of gaining valuable feedback.

As previously mentioned, Post-it notes are a great resource for AfL activities. In the 'on your way out' strategy there are two options that provide the teacher with valuable feedback by asking pupils to write down their thoughts and to post them on the board 'on the way out'.

1. Ask pupils to summarise the lesson so that you know whether the learning objectives have been met. For example, asking pupils 'on the way out write down the three most important bits of information you have learned today' is a useful way to see if what they have written matches the lesson objectives; if not, you have valuable feedback indicating that you may need to revisit the objectives next time.
2. Ask pupils to indicate what they need to more about. For example, asking 'on your way out write down what you think we need to spend more time on because you haven't quite understood the topic' again provides you with valuable feedback to inform the planning of the next lesson.

Taking it further

Divide the whiteboard or a wall into four, with the squares labelled as 'what I enjoyed', 'what I found difficult', 'what I need to know more about', 'what makes no sense'. Again, on the way out, pupils post their Post-it note with the topic that fits into one of the squares; this provides you with valuable feedback. See the online resources for a printable template.

The language of feedback

"Language exerts hidden power, like a moon on the tides."
Rita Mae Brown

It is important to consider not just 'what' but 'how' we feedback to pupils, particularly in public places.

Giving feedback to pupils on a one-to-one basis is often a very personal experience, which can be overwhelming for some children. It is not often that pupils have the full attention of the teacher and they may also not be used to the full attention of an adult in their home life. In addition, whilst feedback is a personal activity it is often done in a public space, such as the classroom, which again can make learners feel uncomfortable at the thought of others listening to both their feedback and their response.

When providing feedback, particularly in public, there are some key points that you should be aware of, which include:

- making the feedback constructive
- making the tone of your voice appropriate for the context
- sitting alongside a pupil rather than hovering above
- avoiding personal remarks, which other pupils can hear.

Some ways to enhance feedback are:

- use gestures such as a nod of the head or smiling to show approval
- ask pupils how they prefer to receive feedback
- allow the feedback to be two way and not just you telling them
- use the one-to-one feedback time to listen and carry out diagnostic assessments.

Hitting the top right corner

"To be effective feedback needs to be clear, purposeful, meaningful, and compatible with students' prior knowledge and to provide logical connections." John Hattie and Helen Timperley

Positive and specific feedback is more likely to have impact than negative non-specific feedback.

It is important to remember that feedback is likely to have greater impact when it is positively framed and provides specific formative advice and guidance (see top right corner of the feedback table below). Conversely, negative feedback that is non-specific is likely to be the least informative feedback (bottom left corner).

Negative feedback and specific   Positive feedback and specific

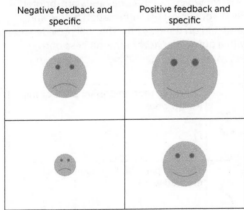

Negative feedback and non-specific   Positive feedback but non-specific

It is also important that pupils understand this concept when providing peer-to-peer feedback. Therefore, display an enlarged version of the feedback table (also available online) to remind everyone about how best to give feedback.

Bonus idea ★

Try giving pupils writing frames to use when providing feedback; this can help them to make it positive and specific. For example, ask them to start their feedback with 'I really liked ... about your work and one area for improvement could be ...'

3-2-1 exit pass

"Teachers systematically and effectively check pupils' understanding throughout lessons, anticipating where they may need to intervene and doing so with notable impact on the quality of learning."
Ofsted school inspection handbook

Plenaries can often be hit and miss. A very simple exercise is the 3-2-1 exit pass, which pupils complete and hand to the teacher on the way out of the lesson.

Plenaries are very much about evaluating the quality of the learning that has taken place, as well as informing planning for the next lesson. This can often descend into chaos, as pupils are busy packing away in preparation for their next lesson. Address this by using the 3-2-1 exit pass, for which pupils complete a pre-printed sheet containing the information below and hand it in on the way out. This will provide you with a quick overview of the success of the lesson, as well as identifying future learning.

Taking it further

The success of the 3-2-1 exit pass depends on you showing that you have taken on board the feedback. A simple way to do this is to start the next lesson with a quick summary of the feedback received, and explain how it is being addressed. For example, this might be by trying to cover more of what pupils indicated they enjoyed or by answering common questions that were asked.

3	The three most important parts of the lesson were: 1) 2) 3)
2	The two parts of the lesson I most enjoyed were: 1) 2)
1	The one question I would like to ask is: 1)

What you need to know about praise

"Much teacher praise is reactive to and under the control of student behaviour rather than vice versa." Jere Brophy

Praise as a form of feedback really does work if given in the right way at the right time!

We all like to be praised, and the rule of thumb related to feedback is that we should praise between four and five times more than we criticise (but this isn't a science). Providing the right amount of praise in the right way is an important strategy to develop, particularly at times when there isn't much to lavish praise about.

Conversely, not all types of praise are good and some types actually appear to have a negative effect on pupils. Some findings from research show:

- Praise works if it is specific, sincere and varied.
- Inflated praise (praise that isn't justified) has varying effects. For children with low self-esteem, it reduces their seeking out of fresh challenges. For pupils with high self-esteem, it increases their expectations of themselves to seek new challenges.
- Personal praise (praise which focuses on personal qualities, such as innate ability) tends to make pupils feel less successful, as a failure in a task was related to a lack of intrinsic ability.
- Process praise has less detrimental effects, as the praise relates to factors that a pupil can control, such as the amount of time allocated to a task.

Teaching tip

Try to consider how much praise you use, and remember the important phrase 'catch them being good' and praising the positive aspects that you see.

Bonus idea ★

Give yourself visual prompts in your lesson plan (or around your room) to remind and encourage you to use praise.

Feedback policy

"A tick or a cross has little impact upon a pupils understanding."

Instead of having a marking policy, consider having a school or departmental feedback policy instead.

There can be confusion around the terms marking, assessment and feedback; the reason for highlighting this is that 'marking' tends to characterise some of the bad practice that can be seen in assessment, particularly related to marking that is merely serving the needs of a school policy rather than meeting the needs of the learner. The reason why marking can, however, be mentioned in the context of AfL is that certain types of marking can be formative so it is not all bad.

Most schools will have a marking policy, which is often very systematic; it should be carried out in a specific way and in a specific timeframe. Whilst some of this pragmatism is understandable, a shift to a feedback policy with an emphasis upon the value, quality and nature of feedback is much more beneficial in terms of achieving a whole-school or departmental commitment to AfL. Therefore a feedback policy might include:

- an overall philosophy of why feedback is important
- information on matching the correct form of feedback to the appropriate activity
- information on the different methods that can be used to provide feedback
- information on the quality of feedback required.

Taking it further

Having a focus on feedback requires a change from frequency (how often) to formative (how detailed). These are big decisions. Any member of staff who will be affected by a new policy should have the opportunity to discuss the policy and have their say in how it is formed, so that there is a shared understanding of any changes, rather than it being seen as an imposed change.

Mini plenaries

"Plenaries should not be considered as the sugar coating of entertainment over the same old learning – they are integral to securing pupils learning."

Plenaries provide valuable two-way feedback opportunities. However, they are often misused or misunderstood.

Did lesson plenaries exist 20 years ago? I don't remember them! They are one of the legacies of the introduction of national strategies, which brought the term into teachers' vocabularies, but in doing so created misconceptions. The most notable of these is that every lesson should consist of three parts, beginning with a starter and ending with a plenary.

Although this is one way of viewing a lesson, the reality is that learning is much more complex than this. If used effectively, plenaries will take place not just once but throughout the lesson.

Within a lesson, regularly monitor and reorientate the pupils. For example, if you are adding layers of complexity throughout the lesson, use a mini plenary prior to each new layer to gain feedback about how much pupils will be challenged by the next target. Of course, an end-of-lesson plenary is still valuable to monitor how well the objectives of the lesson have been achieved.

Teaching tip

Having a plenary at the end of the lesson may be a waste of time as often pupils are distracted and often getting ready for the next lesson. Therefore, if using plenaries use them at the most appropriate time; this is usually immediately after of a learning sequence.

Taking it further

A further misconception is that a plenary has to be a fun game. Although it is desirable to have fun activities, often the fun element can override the learning. A plenary, first and foremost, must meet the requirements of the learning.

DIRT

"Every piece of formative feedback for a pupil should require a response from the pupil, otherwise the feedback wasn't worth it."

It is important to build in reflection time, and that pupils understand what it is for and how it helps their learning.

AfL is as much about identifying what pupils don't know as what they do.

'Dedicated Improvement and Reflection Time' (DIRT) works on the principle that to get the most out of assessment practices there first has to be a commitment to continuous improvement. In order to achieve such improvement, appropriate time should be given to pupils for reflecting upon how to improve.

Therefore try to avoid using feedback to tell pupils where they are (as in a mark out of 10); use it to tell them about how they can improve. Such feedback can be written or verbal, but should be differentiated and focused on the individual. The key is to give the pupils sufficient time to reflect and act on such feedback, both to have the time to physically interpret the feedback but also to engage in a process of metacognition.

Central to DIRT is that feedback is recognised as an important feature of leaning and that appropriate time is given for reflection.

Taking it further

Some teachers have developed ratios to show how much reflection time is needed for students to be able to action feedback; five minutes of verbal feedback equals 25 minutes of reflection time.

If you only have a minute

"In a completely rational society, the best of us would be teachers and the rest of us would have to settle for something less."
Lee Iacocca

Feedback systems need to be manageable and should not simply mean an increase in the teacher's workload. Therefore, the use of common codes and symbols across a department or school can save time.

AfL isn't meant to create a burden for teachers; whilst many of the ideas in this book are about providing high-quality feedback, the trade-off is that teachers should be marking less. Instead of attempting to provide feedback for every book, using a variety of approaches such as self-assessment, peer-assessment and teacher assessment should enable the frequency of teacher assessment to drop.

In some cases this isn't possible, as schools will have rigid marking policies that say that all books have to be marked each week. In such cases it is important that key principles are achieved which include:

- Feedback is quick and frequent.
- Pupils have to respond to feedback.
- Pupils are given time to think and respond.

In such cases a simple three symbol coding system can be used:

- F = Feedback. You will need to see the pupil and discuss their work in the lesson.
- + = Something needs to be added to the work to improve it (this can be linked to a peer-assessment activity). The emphasis is on pupils reflecting upon what they may need to do to improve.
- L = Look back at previous feedback on your work as you still need to work on this.

Taking it further

Any notation system can be used as long as pupils (and parents) understand it. When using such a system it is a good idea to have it pasted into the front of a pupil's exercise book.

Bonus idea ★

Pre-made ink stamps are another way of providing quick feedback to pupils.

From verification to elaboration

"Aerodynamically speaking, bees shouldn't be able to fly – it's just that they haven't been told."

Getting the right balance between verification and elaboration is the key to effective formative feedback.

Feedback should provide two types of information: verification and elaboration. Verification informs the learner to what extent their work is correct and elaboration guides the learner towards an improved response. Getting the balance right is an important part of effective formative feedback.

Providing written feedback to pupils is one of the rituals of being a teacher; we all enjoy it for the first few months, before we hit the reality of losing evenings to providing endless feedback. It can also be disconcerting to provide feedback to pupils but feel that it is having little impact.

Throughout this book, it is emphasised that if feedback isn't having an impact then it probably isn't worth doing. By adopting some of the ideas in this book, your feedback will have greater impact. Central to formative feedback is that it represents information communicated to the learner that is intended to 'modify the learner's thinking or behaviour for the purpose of improving learning'.

Taking it further

Carrying out an audit to find out whether the balance between elaboration and verification is the right balance for you and your pupils is an effective way of improving learner outcomes.

In summary, written feedback should provide:

- Timely information: This will sometimes involve rapid feedback, and at other times the feedback will be delayed. The point is that the timing of feedback is considered.
- Formative information: By its nature, formative feedback should aim to modify the learner's behaviour, thinking and future action.
- Verification information: At the simplest level verification informs the learner if they are correct or not, but to be formative it needs to elaborated on and not merely summative.
- Elaboration information: Elaboration extends verification by discussing the errors, providing or referring to examples and giving guidance on improvement strategies (for example, 'even better if').
- Specific information: Where possible the feedback should be specific to the learner and the context of learning.
- Actionable information: Ultimately, if the feedback cannot be acted upon it is unlikely to have any impact.

Bonus idea

As well as checking the balance is correct in relation to verification and elaboration it is also useful to map these two entities out. For example, you may decide within certain stages of the year or within a project to go for an intense prolonged focus on elaboration followed by shorter periods of verification. There is no one way of doing this but it is important the teacher has a clear view of how the different forms of assessment interact with the learning over time.

Sit next to me

"'Assessment' comes from the Latin word *assidere* which means to 'sit by' or to 'sit beside'."

Keep a note in your register to ensure you take the time to sit next to each pupil at least once during each half term, project or each scheme of work.

Teaching tip

Sitting next to pupils in a lesson can be a challenge for both the teacher and the pupil. You need to consider how they can gain and provide private feedback in a public space without it being intimidating. This includes thinking carefully about your body language, seating position and tone of voice.

As the quote above shows, assessment has its roots in sitting with someone and engaging in dialogue about a planned outcome. In many ways this is the central point of AfL; the dialogue allows the teacher to gain evidence about where the pupil is in their learning in order to help them arrive at where they need to be.

The teacher's role in this isn't simply to tell the learner what to do next. Symbolically, the act of the teacher sitting next to the pupil signifies this as a partnership, with the teacher's role to encourage reflection and self-sufficiency on the part of the learner.

If sitting next to pupils is going to be integrated into your repertoire, plan it so that you sit next to each pupil at the most effective time. You should also ensure that all pupils get an opportunity to sit next to you, not just the most noisy or most demanding. Keep a log in your register across a scheme of a week, a half term or a series of weeks dedicated to a project so that you manage to sit next to each pupil at least once.

Resilience through feedback

"It's not how far you fall, it's how high you bounce when you reach bottom."

Feedback is often difficult to accept, particularly if it is perceived as negative feedback. Learners have to recognise that all feedback is valuable, and how someone responds is the most important aspect of feedback.

Reframing feedback that is perceived as negative allows learners to focus on what matters, rather than being sidetracked on personalities and indifferences.

Although no one likes negative feedback or setbacks, it is how we respond to such setbacks that is most important. The difficulty with feedback is that we take it personally and then will often respond personally. For instance, in research as part of AfL it has been found that children who got a low mark would often not read the feedback provided as they felt it was merely further criticism and added more anguish to the process.

Some children feel that feedback is further evidence of teachers picking on them, all of the time – but the reality is often different. In order for all children to attempt to view negative feedback as a positive way to improvement you should remove personalities from the situation. A process of reframing is necessary to focus on what needs to change and why. Avoid negative or critical feedback where possible, but reframe feedback to pupils as providing the key to unlocking the path to improvement, whilst no feedback or limited feedback keeps the path locked.

Teaching tip

There is one final point to emphasise to learners – most of the time difficult feedback is given by someone because they care, and because they are not willing to take the easy option of merely saying something palatable.

Taking it further

Give pupils examples of successful people who learned from negative feedback. If Michael Jordan had focused on how many times he had missed the basket, he would never have become one of the world's greatest basketball players. If James Dyson had focused on the failed prototypes he had when developing his revolutionary vacuum cleaner, he would never have become one of the world's best-known designers. And if J.K. Rowling had focused on the rejection letters then we wouldn't have Harry Potter.

Feedback loops

"Feedback: the process in which part of the output of a system is returned to its input in order to regulate its further output."

Feedback loops is an engineering term that can be applied to AfL to ensure that feedback creates an impact on the learner.

Teaching tip

An important strategy in teaching is the reducing of pupil dependence on their teacher over time. Therefore, if a pupil always turns to you when they are 'stuck' then you may be missing an opportunity. As such, limiting the amount of additional feedback and thus forcing the pupil to be more proactive in the four stage feedback loop is an effective way to increase a pupil's ownership of learning. This strategy needs to be adapted to the age and ability of the pupils you are working with but the concept of 'reducing dependence over time' should be shared with pupils and parents.

It is mentioned early on in this book that AfL is not an attack on summative assessments. In fact, the use of summative data in a formative way can have a powerful effect on the learner. To encourage learners to be included in the assessment process we can use a four stage feedback loop:

- Stage one: Data collection for example, the marking of a book or a test. Data is collected all the time but unless something useful is done with it, it will have little or no impact.
- Stage two: Relay and relevance. This is providing feedback to the user (the pupil) in a way that will create the most effective means for changing the behaviour. This way the data is presented back to the pupil at an appropriate level to enable them to understand and take action in relation to meeting their targets.
- Stage three: Consequence. This is where the teacher explains how to improve and the different ways that this might be achieved.
- Stage four: Action. This is where the pupil acts on the information by reflecting and improving.

The point about this process is that it makes it clear that feedback isn't just to tell you where you are, but also how you can improve in order for the feedback cycle to continue.

Setting your own targets

"If practices fail to serve the underlying principles such as making learning explicit and promoting learning autonomy, then they cease to be AfL." Mary James

Getting pupils to own their learning targets creates a greater motivation for them to achieve their targets.

In an effort to keep healthy I bought a device that you wear on your wrist that monitors your sleep, how much you eat and how much exercise you get. The feedback it gave me showed that I wasn't getting enough exercise, I wasn't getting the right amount of sleep and I wasn't eating the correct things. Every day I looked at the data I got more despondent, as I was some way off meeting any of the targets.

Then I realised that the targets being set were unreasonable – they were the factory settings and not appropriate for someone my age or lifestyle. I therefore changed the targets to 10% over my average scores. Suddenly I owned the target-setting process by myself; it became much more challenging and I become highly motivated.

The relationship with children's learning is clear – often external targets are neither achievable nor recognisable, and research has consistently shown that intrinsic motivation is much more powerful than externally set targets. In your lessons build in time for pupils to set and negotiate their own targets; it is a really important part of AfL.

Teaching tip

It seems counterintuitive, but pupils often grow increasingly dependent on their teacher during their final years in school when the assessment stakes are getting higher – it is exactly the time we should be reducing their dependency on others and increasing their sense of responsibility.

Bonus idea ★

Setting your own targets is a difficult task. Use pre-printed target cards which pupils can select themselves outlining the target level and the steps to achieve that level of accomplishment; it is a great way of getting pupils to take the lead.

The goal gradient effect

"AfL is about bringing pupils into the learning process."

Extra motivation is gained by knowing where you are on a learning journey, knowing how far you have progressed and celebrating success along the way.

Teaching tip

Start any new activity with a self-assessment so that pupils know they are already on the way, and then identify the clear steps to success and reward – which probably won't be a free cup of coffee!

If you have any loyalty cards, for example, the ones where every time you buy a cup of coffee it counts towards a 'free' cup later on, then you will know that this is an incentive to stay loyal to a particular company as well as a device to encourage you to buy more frequently.

Imagine that with one coffee company you have to get ten stamps on your card to get the final one free, but with another company you have to buy twelve cups of coffee but the first two spaces are already stamped.

With which coffee card do you think you are more likely to get a full set of stamps first?

The tendency is to think that both are the same, as both require ten stamps. However, research has shown that in reality those with two spaces already stamped proceed to complete their collection of stamps faster than those starting from scratch.

Taking it further

With younger pupils you can even create your own loyalty cards, which you stamp as they make progress; they can use self-assessment and peer-assessment against criteria to work out where they are in their learning progress and how many stamps they should get.

This phenomenon is known as the goal gradient effect, and the application to pupils assessment is clear: pupils need to know where they are on their journey of assessment. They also need to know that they are not starting from scratch and their journey needs to be plotted and be an achievable journey.

Public scrutiny

"AfL provides an opportunity to move beyond simple criteria – but requires a shared understanding and definition of the capability to be developed."

Pupils need to be taught how to give and take feedback that is constructive and respectful.

The demands and gains from peer-to-peer scrutiny of work can be considerable but it is worth investing time in establishing how such activities are conducted.

There are inherent obstacles to peer-assessment. If you try to encourage a group of pupils to peer review their work, they may simply refuse to show others their work. Alternatively, you might set up a really interesting peer-assessment exercise, only to find that the pupils see it as an opportunity to be incredibly rude about each other's work.

This illustrates that public scrutiny of work needs to be managed in certain environments, particularly in situations where pupils are not familiar with the protocols of peer-evaluation. Providing pupils with clear expectations about how to feedback is really important.

- Remind pupils that peer review is valuable and important.
- When giving feedback, pupils should aim to be *positive*, *specific* and *thoughtful*.
- Use strategies such as two stars and a wish to help frame responses in a positive way.
- Ensure that feedback is against the criteria and not general.
- Ensure the feedback is on the work and not the person.
- Ask pupils to think about how they would like to receive the feedback they are giving.

Taking it further

Giving and taking feedback is a life skill. It is important to explain to pupils that they are developing such skills, and that they will find them useful for many years to come, and in many different situations.

Feedback sandwiches

"The worst feedback is no feedback!"

Use the feedback sandwich approach to try and provide balanced and constructive feedback.

Teaching tip

Research tells us that saying the same message to two different people can have different interpretations and different impact. Knowing who you are feeding back to is as important as what you are feeding back.

It has been emphasised in this book that it is not just what you give feedback on, but also how you give the feedback that is important. Give feedback the wrong way and you may have wasted your time as it will have little impact.

One way of thinking about giving good feedback is to consider the feedback sandwich, which has two layers with the meaty bit in the middle.

Consider using the following layers when giving feedback:

- Bottom layer (the start of the feedback) – constructive feedback.
- Middle 'meaty' layer (the middle) – what needs to be done to improve for next time.
- Top layer (the conclusion) – positive comment.

Taking it further

When giving feedback, think about the type of response you want to elicit; this will allow you to adapt your feedback appropriately.

Following the basic sandwich recipe ensures a simple constructive framework for feeding back information.

Improving teaching through AfL

Part 3

How not to fail children with AfL

"School is a place where you learn to be stupid." John Holt

Pupils will often use different strategies to avoid being engaged in learning. Get round this using these AfL techniques.

In *How Children Fail*, John Holt details the ways that children work their way through school trying to find the 'route of least resistance' by avoiding engagement with the learning process. Many of the strategies for AfL are based on overcoming the barriers to learning that Holt describes:

- Pupil avoidance strategies – pupils avoid contact with teachers. Central to AfL is targeted engagement with all pupils and the monitoring of individuals.
- Failure incompetence strategy – pupils simply say they 'can't do'. AfL starts from where the learner is and sets targets with the learner.
- Appear to know – pupils pretend they know the answer by putting up their hand knowing they won't be selected. Using the no hands rule and targeted and random questioning means all pupils have to be prepared to answer a question.
- Don't look back, its too awful – a pupil submits a piece of work in the hope it will be okay. Self- and peer-assessment strategies return ownership and accountability back to the pupil.
- Fear of success – pupils simply won't take part as failure is easier to accept if you don't participate. Developing self-esteem is a key feature of AfL, achieved through developing a clear understanding of what quality looks like and how it can be achieved.

Taking it further

For a better understanding of the many strategies that children use to avoid learning read *How Children Fail* by John Holt.

Changing the way that you do it

"Every teacher who wants to practice formative assessment must reconstruct the teaching contract so as to counteract the habits acquired by his pupils." Philippe Perrenoud

AfL often requires us to view the classroom and learning in a different way.

Although many of the ideas in this book are straightforward, some are more difficult to implement than others. AfL isn't simply a series of gimmicks; rather, it is a commitment to a particular way of teaching and learning.

Despite this, many teachers and pupils feel uncomfortable with some aspects of AfL, and some teachers even say that they 'hate AfL'. What they often mean is that they hate feeling vulnerable in changing the way they teach or they hate feeling frustrated about not knowing quite how to get it right.

The same applies to pupils, as they are also asked to work in different ways and may also feel uncomfortable about it.

To work through the discomfort, bear in mind the positive results of successful AfL:

- Pupils change from being passive receivers of information to become active learners.
- Pupils take on more responsibility for their own learning.
- Pupils have the capacity to monitor the quality of their own work during production.
- Teachers shift some of their responsibility to pupils.
- Teachers share the assessment practices rather than keeping them secret.
- Teachers work more strategically and quality assure rather than quality control.

Teaching tip

AfL is more than not giving a number or a grade. It is about helping learners to learn and understand. Therefore emphasis has to be placed on helping pupils become autonomous and reflective learners to ensure that they are not merely passive receivers in the learning process.

59

Praising persistence

". . . constructive feedback from teachers ensure[s] that pupils make significant and sustained gains in their learning." Ofsted school inspection handbook

We need to think about our responses to pupils in order to get the maximum long-term gains.

Possibly the single most powerful force in our existence is the way we feel about and perceive ourselves. Such self-esteem is linked to our sense of worth and is best defined as 'a confidence and satisfaction in oneself'; this is closely related to a person's self-concept, which relates to the 'mental image one has of oneself'. Self-esteem can be considered to be indicative of the value that people place upon themselves.

In AfL we need to consider how feedback is connected with motivation. In many ways, good practice in AfL links naturally with developing learners' self-esteem. Conversely, we know from research that different types of feedback have different impacts on an individual's motivation.

For example, feedback and praise about a person's innate ability has little positive impact, and can have a negative impact. Praising an individual's commitment to a task, perseverance and effort has a greater positive impact upon a learner.

Consider your response to learners who give up on something saying that they 'can't do it' or are 'no good at it'. Often they are reflecting upon their perceived intellectual abilities rather than their ability to face adversity and tackle a challenge. A long-term strategy with great gains is to praise and give regulated feedback related to persistence and 'incremental learning'.

Impact vs cost

"Feedback is one of the most powerful influences on learning and achievement, but this impact can be either positive or negative."
John Hattie and Helen Timperley

The ideal scenario is to identify low cost and high impact teaching and learning strategies.

What is the value of one day's teaching, in terms of financial outlay and payback? This is a tough question and one that is very difficult to disentangle. In times of financial crisis and limited resources we need to know what is worth spending funds on; if we are providing a resource that doesn't have any impact then why is the expenditure being made?

Many would argue that it is impossible to calculate the value of education, and measuring outcome in terms of economic benefit rather than significance to the individual would give a highly skewed view. The good news from research is that, in broad terms, increasing the amount of teaching time outweighs the cost of providing that instruction, and that increased grade performance does lead to increased earnings for pupils in later life.

What type of extra teaching pays dividends in the long run? There some key aspects of AfL that are seen to have greater impact than other aspects of school life.

High impact vs cost	Low impact vs cost
Feedback	Ability grouping
Metacognition	Smaller classes
Collaborative work	After school classes
Peer-to-peer work	Teaching assistants

Teaching tip

As always, a lot will depend upon the specific context, but it is reassuring to know that investing in AfL does have a long-term impact on learners. Use this information to help influence your school's strategy.

Taking it further

For further information about cost compared to impact visit the Education Endowment Toolkit: educationendowment foundation.org.uk/ toolkit/.

Evidence based teaching?

"When dealing with people, remember you are not dealing with creatures of logic, but creatures of emotion." Dale Carnegie

Moving to an evidence based approach towards implementing AfL requires a long-term investment.

Weight Watchers has the philosophy that small habit changes can have a big impact, and this is also true of teachers wishing to improve their teaching through peer-to-peer observations. Unfortunately, peer observations have developed a bad reputation as they often become focused on demonstration of techniques related to the grading of teachers, which can skew behaviour more towards teacher performance than pupil learning. Improving teacher performance takes time and changing habits requires continued effort. This requires a commitment to change, a genuine commitment to pupil learning (and not just performance), a culture of trust and the use of evidence to inform practice.

For ideas to be embedded into a teacher's repertoire, extended practice over time and a willingness to commit to such practice is required. Where possible, such practices should be developed in an informed way and should be part of an evidence based approach. Therefore, rather than relying upon subjective observations alone, data should be collected where possible and used in an informed way.

Evidence based approaches using peer-to-peer observations are about empowering teachers, not simply about catching them out!

Lesson study

"Those teachers most successful with AfL report changing their thinking from how best to cover the curriculum to how best to encourage pupils to learn."

Lesson study is an excellent way of developing AfL.

Whilst peer review and observation tends to focus on individuals and individual performance, lesson study takes a much more collaborative view to developing and improving teaching and learning in the classroom through research and enquiry. Lesson study is where teams of teachers from either a single subject or across different subject areas focus upon an area of AfL, for example, questioning strategies.

The basic principles of lesson study are:

- A group of teachers work together on a long-term goal.
- Collectively the teachers plan and observe a series of lessons focusing upon elements of the long-term goal.
- The teachers plan further research lessons in order to gather data (in different forms).
- A detailed analysis of the emerging data is made.
- Future research lessons are revised and adapted.
- Often the findings of lesson study are disseminated within both schools and wider networks.

Teaching tip

One obvious difficulty with lesson study is getting all the teachers available at the same time to observe a lesson. This was overcome in one school by bringing in a group of pupils on a school training day so that all teachers could participate.

Collaboration contract

"Mark Twain said it is easy to stop smoking – he had done it hundreds of times!"

Many AfL activities require pupils to work collaboratively, and a pupil-generated contract is one way to support such activities.

There is an important distinction to be made between pupils working in groups and pupils working collaboratively. Many of the ideas in this book are specifically about pupils working collaboratively as part of developing their speaking, listening and thinking skills.

Collaboration won't simply happen, so it is worth investing time with learners discussing how to collaborate effectively. One way of doing this is through the generation of a 'collaboration contract' that identifies how pupils will participate and contribute when working within a group. To be most effective, the contract should be created by the group. A 'contract' might take the following format.

Collaboration Contract

Names:

1.

2.

3.

4.

Here are our agreed rules about collaboration:

1.

2.

3.

When we are feeding back to each other we
will _____

_____

When assessing each other's ideas our five
golden rules will be:

1. Respect our partner(s) work because they
   have done their best and so their work
   should be valued.
2. Try to see how they have tackled the learning
   objective and only try to improve things that
   are to do with the learning objective.
3. Tell our partner(s) the good things we see in
   their work.
4. Try to make our suggestions as clear as
   possible.
5. Be fair to our partner(s). We will not talk
   about their work behind their backs because
   we wouldn't like them to do it to us.

Signed by (pupil 1):

Signed by (pupil 2):

Signed by (pupil 3):

Signed by (pupil 4):

Taking it further

It is also important to
establish frameworks
for how pupils should
talk to each other when
providing feedback. For
example, pupils need to
consider what is effective
and appropriate dialogue
when feeding information
back to a partner or peer.
This might include how
to negotiate, providing
feedback sensitively,
effective listening and
using appropriate and
extended vocabularies.

Reducing dependency

"Effective teaching is ultimately making yourself redundant."

The extent to which you as a teacher commit to AfL will be dependent on what you value in teaching and learning.

There is little doubt that learning happens in many different ways and as such there is no one definitive model of teaching or teacher. In fact, there is evidence in certain contexts that removing the teacher altogether can actually increase learning, the reality being that in such circumstances pupils have no choice but to take responsibility for their learning. Clearly this wouldn't work with all pupils or in all contexts but it does present an interesting paradox, as over-reliance on a teacher may be detrimental to long-term success.

Before disappearing from your classroom in the hope that your pupils' results may increase, remember that many pupils and parents will view the teacher-pupil relationship in a traditional way and will expect teaching to be done in a particular way. Nevertheless, a teaching trajectory that seeks to increase pupil autonomy whilst reducing dependency over time should be an overall aim of the teacher. As indicated previously, AfL is not just a series of hints and tips, it is more a philosophy of teaching. Therefore, you should consider what type of AfL teacher you are and how much dependency you wish to create amongst your pupils.

Taking it further

Much of this book has been about increasing pupil reflection yet equally important is the teacher's own reflection on what they believe effective teaching and learning should be. Therefore, taking time to reflect shouldn't be undervalued, likewise taking time to further understand your subject and the community and aspirations of those you teach is equally important. By taking time to consider both your subject knowledge and your pedagogic knowledge and the means to adapt each in the environment that you teach in is an important part of effective AfL.

It is unlikely that all teachers can or will want to increase pupil autonomy over time. Nonetheless, a considered approach is an important element of an overall philosophy of AfL. Considering the questions below and regularly revisiting them will help develop a more informed position:

- In what ways do I believe pupils learn best?
- What AfL strategies do and don't work with my pupils, in my subject, in my school?
- What aspects of AfL would I wish to develop in my teaching repertoire?
- In what areas of learning would I wish to increase pupil autonomy and how do I achieve this over time?
- What mechanisms are there to improve my practice related to increasing autonomy (for example, peer review, coaching, lesson study)?
- What is my timeframe for development?
- What are my next three positive steps to develop my practice in relation to developing pupil ownership and autonomy?

Bonus idea ★

'Praxis' is a useful term to recognise teacher development related to linking theory, practice and reflection. AfL is a good example of praxis in action.

AfL feedback checklist

"Every child knows how they are doing, and understands what they need to do to improve and how to get there. They get the support they need to be motivated, independent learners on an ambitious trajectory of improvement." Department for Children, Schools and Families

Use the table below to identify which approach best describes how you give feedback to pupils.

Teaching tip

Comment only marking has been shown to have a greater impact on learners than giving a grade, a mark or a percentage. However this type of feedback does require the teacher to provide high quality 'perceptive' feedback in order to move the learner on.

Feedback	Always	Sometimes	Never
Comments identify what has been done well and what still needs improvement			
Guidance on how to make improvements is provided			
Feedback is designed to encourage 'thinking' to take place in the learner			
Time is provided for learners to read feedback and to action plan/set targets based upon the feedback			
Opportunities for learners are available (in different ways) for learners to clarify feedback with the teacher/peers			

Feedback	Always	Sometimes	Never
Assessment tasks are related to the criteria and shared with the learners			
Feedback provides a 'scaffold' for improvement			
Feedback is differentiated and tailored to the individual			
Learners are encouraged to reflect on their own performance prior to comments			
Feedback is varied, for example, sometimes one-to-one, group, regular, short, long, etc.			
Feedback is regular and rapid (when appropriate)			
Feedback develops learner autonomy			
SMARTER targets are used (see Idea 86)			

Taking it further

Look to work on those areas that may be underdeveloped on the table if you feel they would benefit the learners in your environment.

AfL and behaviour management

"Are you the kind of teacher that lights up children's faces when you walk in the classroom? Or are you the kind of teacher that when you leave the classroom – children's faces light up!"

By using AfL strategies you will be taking a proactive approach to behaviour management.

If a pupil is determined to disrupt a lesson then there will be little that you can do to stop them – all you have control of is how you respond. However, in many lessons there will be a group of pupils for whom we have an opportunity to make the situation winnable – these are the one's who haven't decided if they are going to participate or disrupt your lesson. Through high quality teaching and learning strategies (in addition to clear structures and routines) we can prevent these pupils from having the opportunity to be disruptive through increasing the level of engagement and challenge in a lesson. Therefore, AfL strategies can be successfully used to address low-level disruption.

Many of the ideas in this book are about high challenge, consideration of motivational factors, increased autonomy and challenge, ownership, collaborative learning and high-level engagement and thinking. In many ways these are also central principles for 'behaviour for learning' (BfL), with AfL and BfL both, unsurprisingly, having a focus on learning.

Much low-level disruption is caused by children being bored, not knowing what to do or being easily distracted. AfL and BfL are both proactive strategies that work on the basis that prevention is better than cure.

QR codes

"QR Code: A machine-readable code consisting of an array of black and white squares, typically used for storing URLs or other information for reading by the camera on a smartphone."

Clever use of QR codes allows feedback to become interactive.

Many schools are increasingly using smartphones, iPods or tablets in lessons as a means of making them more interactive. One particular success story is to use camera technology to read QR codes which can be pasted around the room, in books or attached to particular pieces of equipment to provide a link to a website or video which provides further information. As always, setting up the associated resources may take some time, but some possible applications include:

- QR codes linked to learning objectives – each learning objective has a QR code, which pupils can scan to find further information.
- QR codes linked to pupil videos for the teacher to access – pupils create videos in which they explain the thinking behind, for example, a piece of writing. A QR code is printed by the pupil and pasted into their exercise book for the teacher to scan.
- QR codes linked to further activities or support – as part of your feedback, paste QR codes which link to further online tasks, support materials or resources into pupils' exercise books.
- QR codes can be used to share examples of meeting the criteria. On criteria sheets, include a QR code which leads to model pieces of work or extracts from them.

Teaching tip

As with most technology, the possibilities are endless, but each possibility requires an investment of time. QR codes and other forms of linked technology enable paper-based activities to become interactive and help direct pupils to take on increased responsibility for extending the learning.

Taking it further

Using QR codes is an excellent way of providing subtle differentiation, as QR codes placed in pupils' books can link to differentiated resources to support learning in a specific and targeted way.

Whole-school commitment

"A school where staff ask questions, quote evidence, plan together, observe each other's practice, and talk about teaching and learning, is a good school. It is in effect, a research and learning community." Tim Brighouse.

If AfL is going to be embedded across a department or school then it requires a commitment to ongoing development.

Individual implementation of many of the AfL strategies in this book will not be that demanding, however, if AfL strategies are to be actively used in a school then there really needs to be a whole-department or whole-school commitment to this as part of a strategic approach to its development. Such approaches are critical in sustaining the development of AfL in schools and most importantly embedding it into practice. Key features of good practice include:

- Teachers recognise that AfL is a professional skill and developing this skill requires an ongoing process of commitment and refinement.
- Coaching, peer-observation or lesson study are used as part of a continual dialogue of improvement.
- There is a commitment to ongoing and long-term sustainable improvement rather than attempts at quick fixes.
- Coaching, peer review and lesson study approaches are sensitive to the context of where the development is taking place.
- An ongoing dialogue is developed through staff development and staff meetings, and dissemination of information is maintained.
- Time is taken to recognise progress and celebrate successes.

Taking it further

Ensure that AFL is a standing item on the agenda of meetings is a way of keeping AfL a priority. It is equally important to build AFL into school and departmental development plans with clear targets, which are monitored. Finally, ensuring that there is an opportunity to share good practice and learn from each other through coaching and mentoring is a further way to ensure AfL is embedded and sustainable within a school.

Differentiation in AfL

"Good teaching forces differentiation." Phillippe Perrenoud

Differentiation is embedded in the philosophy of AfL.

Differentiation implies that the teacher is doing something intentional and deliberate. Therefore, differentiation is about the planning and activities that teachers employ to accommodate the individual differences that learners have.

Many teachers struggle with the concept of differentiation, but understanding AfL principles should address some of this confusion. It stands to reason that if you are teaching a whole class in the same way at the same time then you are probably not differentiating your teaching, and as a consequence not teaching formatively. There may be valid reasons for such approaches, although I can't think of many!

AfL strategies force the teacher to differentiate their teaching and many of the ideas in this book are about differentiation in action. This may be achieved through differentiated:

- planning
- learning objectives
- questions
- feedback from pupil to teacher and teacher to pupil
- vocabulary
- explanations
- emotions and gestures
- resources
- tasks
- grouping of pupils
- use of praise
- listening.

> **Teaching tip**
>
> Differentiation is not about closing the gap between learners, it is about the difference between where a learner is in their learning and where he or she has the potential to be.

Emotional literacy and AfL

"Teacher: 'What is it with you – ignorance or apathy?' Pupil: 'Don't know – not really bothered!'"

Effective teaching is about being emotionally literate.

One of the central messages in this book is about providing feedback to pupils. Within this context it is important to consider the 'emotional' language (both body and voice) that we use when feeding back to pupils.

Creating the right 'emotional climate' is central to any effective classroom. Some teachers are instinctively strong in this area and are able to adjust their teaching according to their pupil's emotional needs. Such emotional literacy is not always natural, however, so some teachers can get it wrong and as a result undermine their teaching and pupil learning. This is particularly true in areas relating to assessment and feedback as many pupils feel vulnerable in the assessment process. You can acknowledge the emotional aspects of the classroom by:

- being aware of pupils' emotional needs
- adapting verbal feedback, for example, tone and choice of words
- adapting body language, for example, gestures
- framing activities by acknowledging emotional demand, for example, 'you may feel nervous'
- acknowledging your own and your pupils' feelings
- modelling behaviours and emotions
- creating an emotionally safe environment where pupils feel they can share their thinking
- creating trusting relationships over time.

Design not planning

"Everyone designs who devises courses of action aimed at changing existing situations into preferred ones." Herbert Simon

Shifting from the planning of a lesson to the design of a lesson offers increased opportunities for refining the effectiveness of lessons over time.

Lesson plans are often seen as a necessary chore, often because they are part of a formal requirement, used as part of performance management or preparation for inspection. One of the problems with planning is that of providing sufficient detail to convince the observer of the worth of the lesson.

Lesson planning provides a mental rehearsal for the challenges of a lesson, and a run through of the key episodes. However, there is an important distinction between 'planning a lesson' and 'designing a lesson'.

Planning tends to be a linear process – the lesson is planned from the start to the end and that is it. Conversely, design is an iterative process – the lesson goes through a number of design iterations in order to come up with the best lesson possible in relation to teaching, learning and assessment. This means that the lesson isn't just about getting from A to B, but about getting there in the most interesting way encompassing a range of AfL strategies.

Lesson design therefore involves a continuous cycle of improvement (linked to the lesson study principle); lessons are honed and improved over time rather than simply repeated.

Teaching tip

'When teachers start from what it is they want students to know and design their instruction backward from that goal, then instruction is far more likely to be effective.' *Understanding by Design*, (Wiggins and McTighe, 2000).

Taking it further

Sharing lesson plans/designs electronically (for example, through Dropbox) amongst teachers is an effective way of sharing good practice. However, co-planning/designing lessons is a much more effective way of developing a shared understanding of teaching, learning and assessment in a department or school.

Time for a TIF

"The purpose of education for all children is the same; the goals are the same. But the help that individual children need in progressing towards them will be different." Warnock Report

Triple impact feedback (TIF) recognises that the teacher's role in feedback can vary by the stage at which they are involved.

Central to AfL is that pupils take increased ownership and become more autonomous, demonstrated through pupils being engaged in self-assessment and peer-assessment processes. This will take time to achieve, and the teacher has an important role in monitoring the quality of self- and peer-assessment.

The teacher is just one part of a TIF process. The teachers' position as part of TIF can vary from being at the start, the middle or the end of the process. For example:

1. Teacher: feeds back on pupil work.
2. Pupil: addresses the feedback and then self-assesses.
3. Peer: pupils engage in peer-assessment of the self-assessment.

1. Pupil: self-assesses own work for example, explains how they have met the criteria and what aspects of work they are pleased with.
2. Peer: peer-assessment of the self-assessment.
3. Teacher: feeds back on quality of self- and peer-assessment (provides feedback on the feedback).

1. Peer: peer-assessment of an activity.
2. Teacher: feeds back on quality of peer-assessment (provides feedback on the feedback).
3. Pupil: acts on the feedback and self-assesses at the end of the process.

With great effect

"We all seek positive evidence in that which we love."

Knowing about 'effect size' can help you identify which aspects of AfL have the biggest impact on learners.

How do we know which aspects of our teaching are the most effective? Whilst we may have an intuitive feel for what works and what doesn't, what evidence can we draw upon to give us a better idea of where we should be placing our effort?

More and more teaching is being pushed towards becoming an evidence-based profession, and one way that teachers can increase their understanding is through looking at the research on 'effect sizes'. If we compare two or more intervention groups, effect sizes tell us which one is likely to have a greater effect on the learner.

At this point, some warnings have to be given. Firstly, almost everything a teacher does has some effect (which can also be a negative effect) on a learner. Secondly, trying to isolate the individual aspect of a teacher's repertoire that is creating the effect is quite difficult.

Finally, effect size often works by drawing upon multiple studies and effectively provides an average of those studies. Whilst a particular intervention (for example, group work) might have a significant effect size, there might be some cases where it had no effect. Therefore, although effect size gives a degree of confidence that something might have some impact, there is no guarantee, largely because you are dependent upon a whole host of other variables being correct.

Taking it further

An effect size of 0.4 or above is seen as important, above 0.6 is certainly of some significance and 1.0 or above is significant to the point that the effect is the equivalent to two GCSE places, for example, moving from a grade C to a grade A. One of the most significant findings is that effective feedback, a key aspect of AfL, has an effect size of 1.3. Questioning, peer-assessment, and clarifying goals (all central to AfL) all have an effect size of above 0.4.

Emergency AfL toolbox

"Operator – give me the number for 911." Homer Simpson

Having a set of AfL resources available means you can revert to different strategies even when they were not planned.

Teaching tip

Often when you introduce aspects of AfL to a group for the first time they won't understand what you are trying to do. It is important to persevere with what may seem like alien concepts to some learners.

Most of the activities in this book require some pre-planning and a considered approach. However, life isn't always like this and sometimes in-lesson events transpire that require an immediate response to capitalise on the learning.

This is where the emergency AfL toolkit comes in. It is a range of materials that can be used for organising a class and can help save the day. The toolkit could contain:

- A stack of red and green cards (enough for one for each pupil), for mini plenaries or end-of-lesson plenary: Green = YES, Red = NO.
- Post-it notes, for quick feedback, plenary tasks, on the way out exercises.
- Mini whiteboards, for feedback which requires more than a yes or no.
- Twitter sheets, to be filled in with 140 word summaries of the learning (see Idea 41).
- Exit passes, with 3 questions to answer and hand in to the teacher at the end of the lesson (see Idea 36).

Find further ideas for the toolkit in the online resources.

Teachers as researchers

"Evidence is no substitute for values."

Teachers can collect evidence in simple ways that can have a significant impact on their teaching.

Examining the outcome of an implementation is a good way of finding out whether or not something has been successful. Many teachers view research in the wrong way; my view of research is best described as a systematic way of finding something out: it is planned and there is going to be some evidence to discuss.

An example of this could be as follows:

- Read up on effective questioning from a range of valid sources (the point being that not all sources are valid).
- Plan a strategy for starting to ask higher-level questions in your lessons.
- Audio record a lesson using a small lapel microphone and audio recorder (check school policy that this is acceptable).
- Get the audio transcribed or do it yourself.
- Cut out (or copy and paste) and place your questions into different categories, for example, low- and high-level questions, Socratic questions, procedural questions, use of wait time, etc.
- Reflect on whether the distribution of the questions is what you were aiming for.
- Repeat, or go back to the literature.

This type of approach is iterative and it does not try to draw correlations between questioning and outcomes (which would need a longer study). It simply aims to improve practice. This is best described as an entry-level approach, but it also produces valuable evidence to reflect upon.

Teaching tip

Evidence-based teaching is not simply passing on research for teachers to implement. It is about teachers being discerning and making professional judgements based upon the evidence they have access to.

How much time should I spend on AfL?

"Less is often more!"

There are several important methods that can be used to reduce the time it takes to maintain AfL strategies whilst maintaining quality.

The government's teacher workload survey in 2013 found that teachers spend between 72% and 84% of their working time outside of school on planning, preparation and assessment. Teachers also indicated they spend around ten hours a week specifically on assessment. Clearly this is taking up a significant amount of teachers' time and is worth getting right.

Whilst the proverbial advice to work smarter is the equivalent of telling someone who is drowning to use butterfly stroke, there are some strategies that can make our lives more manageable:

- Increase pupil responsibility. This has pitfalls and is difficult, but it has a double impact in freeing up your time and 'upskilling' pupils.
- Assess less frequently. It is part of the mantra of schools to assess more, but assessing less and increasing the quality of assessment is likely to increase impact.
- 'Upskill' and inform parents. Many parents simply won't understand AfL strategies, so explaining what they are and how they can help their children will be beneficial.
- Use codes and shorthand. Agreeing a set of shorthand comments and codes can save time. It is, however, important to get the balance right; if feedback is to have greater impact it should be formative.

- Use peer-assessment. If you develop a strategy to feedback on the quality of feedback then peer-assessment will have a much greater impact.
- Share criteria. The clearer the criteria the more likely pupils are to meet them.
- Sample. If work has been self-assessed and peer-assessed effectively then taking a sampling approach at key intervals – with all pupils being part of the sample over time – can save time.
- Assess half the work. Often when assessing pupils' work you are repeatedly making the same points. Therefore, only assess half the work and ask pupils to self-assess the other half based upon the initial feedback.

Bonus idea

The new technology built into smart phones and tablets means that teachers can now develop optical marking type systems very quickly and cheaply. Apps such as 'quickkey' allow the teacher to quickly scan pupil's work whilst talking to them and then provide instant formative feedback.

When more pain equals little gain

"Marking is usually conscientious but often fails to offer guidance on how work can be improved." Ofsted general report on secondary schools

Less may sometimes be more in terms of the frequency and quantity of feedback.

Teachers are often incredibly diligent and frequently regard extreme effort and conscientiousness as a badge of honour. Whilst no one would deny these are honourable characteristics, unfortunately they often represent misdirected effort as the gain from the pain is insufficient.

Take the act of marking. Many schools have policies indicating that every class has to have homework set and feedback given to the pupils once a week. Whilst this may seem a sensible policy, assessment is distorted into merely marking the pages, with feedback often being of little value and as a consequence being 'insufficiently used to inform subsequent work'. As a result, the feedback is of little value and the distributed effort across lots of different classes is dissipated.

The alternative is a much more informed approach whereby instead of quantity you emphasise the quality of feedback. For example, if you reduce the amount (per head) of marking from eight groups to two groups per week, but increase the quality of feedback significantly, then the gain should be greater. This doesn't mean the other groups are neglected; their turn for quality feedback will come (approximately every four weeks), and in the interim high-quality self- and peer-assessment should be used.

Taking it further

If you decide to change your approach to the one described here, it is really important that parents understand your reasons and that the benefits are for their children. Sharing such information through parents' evenings and newsletters is a vital way of emphasising that assessment works in many different ways and that, ultimately, changes are about improving their child's learning.

Increasing pupil ownership, autonomy and success through AfL

Part 4

Clear learning objectives

"My sole objective today is to survive this lesson!"

Think about using questions instead of the usual learning objectives that are shared with pupils.

Taking it further

Differentiation can also be built into the above by saying 'here are a couple of additional really tricky questions that some of you may be able to answer once you have answered the first three questions'.

There is nothing duller than teachers reading out learning objectives at the start of the lesson, particularly when they feel they have to. Sharing a learning objective will have no impact unless pupils see it as meaningful and can understand what it is for. If you are reading out learning objectives at the start of a lesson but don't know why then don't do it!

Some teachers struggle with the concept of writing learning objectives, and this is not surprising given that there are often theoretical debates about what constitutes a good learning objective. A simple way of ensuring that a learning objective is valuable and focused is by presenting the learning objectives to pupils as a series of questions.

For example, you can introduce a lesson by saying 'here are three questions that you won't be able to fully answer at present, but you will be able to answer them by the end of the lesson'.

Bonus idea ★

Use Idea 36 3-2-1 exit pass as a means to evaluating the success of the strategy.

Whilst this may not appear significant, it is quite a sophisticated strategy because it shares the learning, identifies progress needed and identifies the success by which the lesson can be judged.

Objective top ten

"If you can't express what the learning should be in a precise and clear way then it is unlikely your teaching will be precise or clear."

A checklist of ten questions to see how effectively you use learning objectives.

Use the following checklist to consider how effective you are when using learning objectives:

1. Are the objectives and outcomes displayed throughout the lesson, so the learners can see the learning focus and outcomes?
2. Do you regularly return to the objectives throughout the lesson, signposting which objective is currently being delivered?
3. Is the lesson delivered in chunks/learning episodes based upon each objective?
4. Are the objectives and outcomes written using appropriate language suitable for the age of the learner?
5. Are signals sent from the teacher to learners when moving from one objective to another?
6. Are objectives expressed in terms of learning and not doing?
7. Are the outcomes expressed as what learners will be able to do as a result of the learning?
8. Has the criteria for assessing the outcomes been shared, discussed, negotiated or highlighted?
9. Are learners involved in generating quality criteria for meeting the objectives?
10. Has space been created for learners to self-assess or peer assess their achievement against the objectives?

Keeping motivated

"I have never met a pupil who isn't motivated – it is just that they are often not motivated in the areas you want them to be."

Intrinsic motivation is more effective than external rewards.

A lot of the ideas in this book require pupils to take on extra responsibility for their learning. For this to be successful they have to be sufficiently motivated to do so. In this context, repeated studies have shown that intrinsic motivation is a much more effective motivator than extrinsic motivation. This means that learners are more likely to be motivated by valuing what they are learning (intrinsic) rather than by achieving a certain level of attainment (extrinsic).

A pupil is more likely to be motivated though a love of a subject rather than the grade that they can get in that subject. Equally, a pupil is more likely to be motivated to improve through AfL strategies if they enjoy a subject than if they are purely pursuing of a grade (although in some situations that can be a motivator). Research has shown that those pupils who viewed assessment as helping them become better learners achieved greater outcomes than those pupils who were dependent upon their teachers for assessment guidance.

Self-efficacy

"What people think, believe, and feel affects how they behave."
Albert Bandura

Increasing pupils' self-belief in their ability to complete a task will increase their perseverance and success in the task.

A key feature of AfL is the developing of pupil's self-efficacy, which is defined as how capable a pupil feels of succeeding in a learning task. Pupils with a positive self-efficacy tend to achieve more, are more resilient and will often persevere with a task for longer. This therefore relates to how information is passed back to a pupil in the form of feedback. Formative feedback is much more likely to be effective if the motivational impact is considered and the focus remains on helping pupils achieve progress in their targets.

Strategies for supporting pupils' self-efficacy in the assessment process include:

- Use short-term and specific targets that are both challenging and attainable.
- Get pupils to talk (with the teacher or partner) through their targets and to maintain a record of their progress.
- Ask pupils to focus on their progress in their targets as opposed to progress compared to other pupils.
- Use positive language such as 'you can do this' and keep the feedback focused on progress against the target.
- Encourage peer-to-peer support, particularly getting peers talking about how they have achieved success by acting upon feedback.

Teaching tip

In order to achieve success pupils need to see and feel what success looks like. Seeing pupils of similar ability achieve success is a useful strategy to employ.

Taking it further

When planning tasks it is important to try to build in early success, as pupils are more likely to persevere if they feel that they are making progress.

AfL beyond the school gates

"Most of our learning is not the result of teaching." John MacBeath

AfL is an important collection of skills that have relevance beyond the classroom.

Teaching tip

Skills such as peer-assessment, providing effective feedback, identifying success criteria and metacognition are as essential outside the classroom as they are inside the classroom!

As humans, there is a limitation to how much raw fat we can eat before we reject it and can't take any more. The same applies to raw sugar; we can only take so much before we revile against it. However, when fat and sugar are combined we can consume almost unlimited amounts, as one appears to offset and complement the other.

I liken this to AfL in that assessment and learning by themselves are both limited and if you have too much of either by itself you can become opposed it. However, by combining 'assessment' and 'learning' as part of 'AfL' we have unlimited opportunities for embedding AfL in our teaching.

Taking it further

It is important that time is taken to explain to pupils how AfL is a lifelong skill that will help them beyond school into higher education and work life.

One important reason to do this is that the skills of AfL represent transferable skills and concepts. AfL is therefore not simply about a short-term goal of passing the next test or a gimmick that creates a positive impression when a teaching is being observed – it is something that develops autonomy that will have significant value beyond the classroom.

Educating parents

"What parents do is more important than who the parents are!"

Explaining to parents what AfL is and how it might be different is an important strategy in getting parents to support their child's learning.

Parents love traditional marking, so some areas of AfL may seem nonsensical or wrong to those who are not familiar with the rationale. This means that it is vital to communicate to parents how AfL works and the thinking behind it and what differences they may see as a parent. For example, they may see books marked in a different way or their children might talk about how their lessons are 'different'.

Explaining these differences might not be straightforward. Nevertheless, all parents want the best for their children and therefore it has to be carefully and repeatedly explained that any changes that are brought in as a result of AfL are in the best interest of their children and that AfL is not some fad.

Explaining AfL to parents might take place through newsletters, open evenings or sample lessons, and getting parents to 'buy in' to the principles will be an important part of the success of AfL in a school. In fact, the more parents can be involved in all aspects of their child's education the better, but they have to be educated to understand that aspects of teaching may be different to their own experiences of education.

Teaching tip

Research shows that parents have a significant impact on pupils' achievement and there are significant benefits to be had through involving parents in their child's education.

Taking it further

Having a key contact for parents, or a section on AfL that can be shared via the school's virtual learning environment or network, is a useful strategy for any school committed to developing AfL principles.

PIES

"A challenge for AfL – pupils should work as hard as the teacher!"

Teachers can sometimes feel disappointed at the end of a lesson because they couldn't have worked any harder, but pupils' learning and productivity has been relatively modest.

Teaching tip

Print out large statements or project the PIES expectations onto a whiteboard so that during the lesson you can keep reminding pupils of their responsibility and expected way of working.

One structure for achieving learner autonomy and ownership, and reducing dependency, is the PIES approach. Based around four areas, the PIES approach works on the principle of maximum and equal participation and responsibility. The structure and ground rules needs to be shared and understood and built into a repertoire of teaching that includes:

- **P**ositive Interdependence (a structured activity that requires a group to complete the task).
- **I**ndividual Accountability (individual contribution with the task is also identifiable and accountable).
- **E**veryone Participates (all contribute and takes turns).
- **S**imultaneous Interaction (all pupils are active – either through speaking or listening).

This means that anyone working in a group cannot hide and there is both an individual accountability and group responsibility based upon equal participation.

PIES comprises an encouragement of AfL principles combined with a strategy that enhances collaborative learning (not group work) in a more advanced way by encouraging participation strategies.

Flight paths not motorways

"Pupils will not all learn in the same way on the same day at the same time!"

Considering pupils' learning as 'flight paths' recognises that learning is often not linear and the route from A to B may not always be straight.

An interesting way of considering pupils learning and assessment is to consider car and aircraft flight paths as an analogy for the different trajectories that pupils will experience. A car on a motorway it will mainly take you from A to B in a straight line, and whilst there may be small detours the path is largely linear with some variations in speed.

A plane, on the other hand, might use different routes and travel at different heights and speeds to get from A to B. Comparing this with learning, we still know that we want to get the pupil from A to B, but we also know that that progress is unlikely to be linear as individual pupils will progress at different rates and have different journeys, and as a result intervention will be needed. Because the path is recognised as not linear, many more checks have to take place to find out where the pupil is, where they need to go to next and how best to get them there.

Mapping student progress in this way is a good example of the formative use of summative assessments. Individual progress scores (tracking points) are monitored and used to adjust the pupil trajectory. As such, progress is monitored and intervention adjusted accordingly.

Explain what really matters

"Formative assessment is central to effective teaching and, by engaging students in it as active participants, the effect is multiplied." Gibbs and Simpson

It is vital that all pupils realise that they have to know the criteria against which they are being judged.

To many pupils it can come as a surprise that they should be increasingly autonomous and should take ownership of their learning. This is no surprise when we see how often children are 'spoon fed'. Schools should be about decreasing pupils dependency on teachers, not increasing it. A way to get the message across is to explain to pupils that they have a responsibility to understand how they assessed and what criteria they are assessed against.

A simple exercise to demonstrate this is as follows:

- Ask pupils to draw a house.
- Ask pupils to give themselves a mark or grade for the house.
- Get pupils to swap their work with their partner.
- Show a marking scheme that gives marks for the various components for a house in the Philippines that is designed from sustainable materials and built to increase ventilation in a tropical environment.

The point of the exercise is to illustrate that we all carry around in our head what we think is the correct answer to a question, even when we don't fully understand the question. Understanding the criteria by which we are assessed is really important.

Taking it further

Although telling pupils the criteria they are being judged against is important, it is also important to ask pupils to think what criteria they think they will be judged against. They will not always be in the fortunate position of being told the criteria, so they also need to be able to consider what criteria may be used to assess them.

Quality assured not quality controlled

"Quality **control** makes sure the results of what you've done are what you expected. Quality **assurance** makes sure you are doing the right things, the right way."

Summative assessment is a quality control system; it checks at the end of the process that what you hoped would happen has happened. Quality assurance ensures you build quality into the system so you don't have to be so reliant upon quality control summative assessments.

One might expect that an aircraft engine factory would have high-quality control systems in place. You might be astonished to find that many don't use quality control processes, as these tend to shift responsibility to someone to find something wrong rather than ensuring accountability is maintained by all to ensure everything is right.

In many ways this is the central feature of AfL and if it is good enough for aircraft engines then it's good enough for pupils learning.

Therefore quality assurance in AfL recognises and increases learning responsibility and autonomy during the learning process by removing the safety net that many learners become dependent upon. This means that end of activity summative assessments are less important than ongoing assessment. Schools, departments and teachers using quality assurance processes constantly ask 'how do we get it right?' rather than asking 'how did it go wrong?'

Teaching tip

Quality assurance in teaching is achieved by adjusting the teaching and learning in real time rather than at the end of a process. Waiting for the results of examinations may provide valuable information for the teacher's teaching in the next cycle – but is too late to have an impact on the learners in the previous cycle.

Taking it further

Attempting to improve quality assurance in teaching and learning can be done in many effective ways including using pupil panels (expert witness), peer-observation, coaching and continued professional development. One example is to ask pupils what aspects of AfL they find unhelpful or beneficial and how it can be improved.

Flipping assessment

"If you are not learning, I am just talking."

Flipping assessment is a way of rethinking how and when we assess pupils.

Flipped classrooms have gained a lot of attention in recent years. The key principles are that valuable lesson time is often lost due to activities taking place in the classroom in the company of a teacher when they could be completed at home or elsewhere. This could be watching a video of a demonstration, listening to a podcast from the teacher or reading some essential material at home. Moving these activities out of the classroom frees up teaching time within a lesson, allowing more focused activities and increased differentiation and encouraging more creative approaches to teaching.

This can also be extended to assessment, and in many ways AfL lends itself to flipped classrooms. It does, however, need to be planned for; this might include:

- Thinking about what assessment currently takes place in the lesson that could take place outside the lesson. For example, key questions that pupils could work on outside of the classroom or self-assessment activities that could be completed elsewhere.
- In the lesson, thinking about assessments that are best conducted in that environment such as peer-assessment and teacher feedback.
- Thinking about the use of technology such as blogs, wikis, pupil podcasts and videos as a further means of assessment.

Rubric placemats

"Rubric: information listing specific criteria for grading or scoring tests or academic work."

Pupils should be assessed against objectives and agreed criteria, which are shared and available to learners.

Self-assessment is central to AfL. Whilst it is a fairly straightforward concept, getting pupils familiar with what they should be self-assessing against isn't always so straightforward. One very simple idea is to use personal named placemats. The placemats are ideally A3 laminated sheets that contain the assessment rubric (and additional spaces), which have either been developed internally or produced by the exam board.

Because these are personal placemats they can be placed in front of pupils at the start of each lesson, allowing them to become increasingly familiar with the criteria against which they are assessing themselves.

Placemat self-assessment activities can be extended by:

- using markers to identify where they are in their self-assessment
- pupils marking where they were at the start of a lesson and at the end (showing progress)
- having a separate target box on the placemat for pupils to record their next steps
- using different colour markers to enable peer-assessment
- taking snapshots with a camera or photocopying the placements to show progress over time.

Teaching tip

As well as pupils having access to criteria, they also need to know what the criteria mean. Having discussions about what the criteria may mean, as well as having examples of work that meets the criteria, will help pupils in their own self-assessments.

Taking it further

Get pupils to use highlighter pens or highlight their work on screen to show where they have met the criteria.

Assessment for development

"Good teaching can overcome bad testing."

Whilst assessment for learning is important, assessment for development may be even more important.

Of all the many diverse areas of the various national strategies over the last 20 years, AfL probably remains the area to generate the most enthusiasm and interest, as well as being one of the few areas of research that could be seen as directly feeding into practice.

Nonetheless, the approaches to AfL have often been misunderstood and frequently reduced to a set of tools without a clear rationale of how to use them. A further concern is also related to the 'learning' aspect of AfL, as what learning actually is remains far from clear. If learning is perceived in a very narrow way then, no matter what strategies are employed, the results will always be inadequate.

A possible solution draws upon the famous psychologist Vygotsky, whose theory of the zone of proximal development (ZPD) has changed the way we think about learning. Note that his theory is on 'development' and not just learning. Moving towards assessment for development (AfD) is a genuine attempt to reconcile the difficulties associated with learning. So what is the difference?

Development is concerned with bringing about desired change in the learner for the benefit of the learner. It takes a much broader view of the learner and considers the changes to be developed in the learner – so learning is nothing without development. There may be subtleties in the distinction but development considers the learner and the learning in a context rather than learning as an isolated act.

As such, moving towards AfD considers learning in a much more developed way and considers learning in terms of the learner's longer term needs. Examples of AfD are probably best characterised by special needs learning, but in reality should be the focus of all learning.

When thinking about development instead of just learning, we have to consider the stage of learning (progression), the level of learning (differentiation), the context of learning (why and where) and the value of learning (will it be useful). In addition, we must think about the big picture and how everything connects with this. Therefore the big picture can be a whole school issue or be a subject issue or a whole year issue. The point is to add value to the learning to develop something else (bigger) than the learning. For example, if a whole school focus was on a strong developmental theme of sustainability then the assessment of the development would be whether the school produced sustainable, environmentally aware pupils – not whether they could pass an examination on sustainability (which they might but which isn't the focus).

Taking it further

Focusing upon development provides an opportunity to move beyond limited criteria to achieve something more than passing examinations. It is about developmental gains within a stronger and more valuable learning context. Therefore, for example, the benefits of learning in mathematics, physics or English would have a stronger focus on the learner benefits related to their development as a person as well as promoting the learning content.

Assessment of, as, or for learning?

"Using one assessment for a multitude of purposes is like using a hammer for everything from brain-surgery to pile-driving."
Walt Haney

AfL is just one 'umbrella' approach to assessment that links with other ways of thinking about assessment.

Teaching tip

Central to any view of assessment is having a shared, clear and explicit view of what success and progress look like.

Hopefully by now you have got a pretty good understanding of AfL. It is useful to quickly distinguish between other approaches to assessment, which are all part of an effective teachers toolkit.

- Assessment for Learning (AfL): In assessment 'for' learning the emphasis is ongoing, real time, formative feedback. It empowers the learner to be active and not just passive in the assessment process. Feedback is embedded in the learning.
- Assessment of Learning (AoL): In assessment 'of' learning the focus is on summative processes such as marks and grades as the means to measuring progress and feedback. Feedback follows the learning.
- Assessment as Learning (AaL): In assessment 'as' learning it is recognised that assessment is part of the learning and what is assessed is the learners ability to identify the correct assessment approaches to improve their own learning. Feedback is through reflection on own learning.

Whilst this book is about AfL, it does not detract from other forms of assessment that make up a balanced approach to teaching, learning and assessment.

Feedback for motivation

"Learners must ultimately be responsible for their own learning since no-one else can do it for them." Assessment Reform Group

Encouraging pupils to develop a 'growth mindset' can be achieved using AfL principles.

Carol Dweck's 'attribution theory' considers how children attribute their failures and successes in different ways. In doing this she has identified two types of response.

First there are those children who have a fixed belief about their ability, and who consider that what they can do is down to some fixed potential (for example, IQ).

Second, there are the children who believe they have untapped ability and that the way to achieve success is through effort and application.

Clearly, those who believe in a fixed ability (the research indicated almost half of the children in their sample) need to be encouraged to shift their thinking. Equally, it has been shown that teaching that had the greatest effect on learners' 'mindset' focused on educating pupils about their learning.

There are some key strategies in relation to this, which include:

- Avoid person-focused praise and feedback such as 'you're very good at this', as this reinforces a fixed ability mindset by referencing innate ability.
- Instead use process-focused praise or praise the application of an individual such as 'that was a good way to attempt the solution' or 'you tried really hard and persevered'.

Teaching tip

Carol Dweck's 'mindset' research encourages teachers to emphasise that ability can be cultivated and that effort is required for learning. Therefore, teachers should praise the progress being made as a result of the additional effort rather than the innate ability to do something.

Taking it further

Carol Dweck is a well-known professor of psychology who has worked extensively on understanding children's motivation. For further information on her theories, read her book *Mindset: How You Can Fulfil Your Potential.*

Setting SMARTER targets

"Setting targets makes you focus on what children are actually learning, not what you think you are teaching." Ofsted

When setting targets it is important that they are clear and that pupils can both understand them and act upon them. This can be achieved using the SMARTER targets acronym.

SMARTER targets provide valuable short-term goals and feedback which can be used to help monitor and identify learning needs. Central to this is pupil ownership of the process and the development of their responsibility of managing their own learning.

Specific	Exactly and precisely state what you want the learner to be able to do, act upon, learn.
Measurable	The measure will be used to indicate when the target is met. Measurable can be quantifiable or descriptive in terms of a shared understanding of quality.
Achievable	Perhaps the most important aspect of a target is that it should be set with the learner in mind to be of sufficient demand without being too demanding. This will usually be based on data and information on prior performance.
Realistic and recognisable	This relates to the making the target achievable. The learner must be able to understand the target, therefore the language of the target has to be correct. Equally, the target must be achievable within the timeframe and ability of the learner.

Time focused	The timeframe for achievement of the target must be clear, whether this is a single episode within a lesson or an extended period of learning over several months.
Evaluated	It is important that the learner and the teacher evaluate targets. The learner may do this through self- and peer-evaluation. The teacher should reflect on the success of the target-setting process and the extent to which the targets were met.
Rewarding	Meeting targets should be rewarding. This means that the targets set should be recognised as valuable and meeting the targets should be recognised using appropriate reward systems.

Taking it further

Pupils setting their own SMARTER targets will increase their motivation and determination. This will often involve negotiation and practice but ultimately pupils should be in control of the targets they set.

'Quality' and 'not so good'

"Self-evaluation is the ability to recognise good work and to correct one's performance so that better work is produced."

It is important to spend time developing an agreed understanding with pupils and colleagues about what 'quality work' looks like.

Teaching tip

Intelligence has been defined as resilience, resourcefulness, reflectivity and responsibility – the very principles upon which AfL is based.

What do we mean by quality work? Often teachers and their pupils can be overly impressed by the neatness of work or the quantity of work produced, but fail to reward innovate or creative work which may be neither neat nor of significant quantity. Coming to a shared understanding with pupils and colleagues of what we value in terms of quality is an important part of AfL.

In relation to this, research has shown that giving students time in a lesson to discuss what 'quality work' may look like and how the work will be assessed can have a significant impact upon learners' achievement. A term that is often used for this relates to what Guy Claxton calls a 'nose for quality'. This relates to the point that learners really need to be able to have an instinctive feel for what good quality means.

Taking it further

One way to develop a shared view of 'quality' is through celebration and awards, such as a monthly best piece of extended writing or best art or design work. The piece of work that is selected should represent quality, and the accompanying narrative should highlight the reason *why* it represents quality.

To help develop pupils' application of the criteria, give them opportunities to look at different samples of work from other pupils and assess it against shared criteria.

Teachers also need to have a nose for what quality looks like, and this means having regular discussions with colleagues, within individual departments and professional networks, of what 'quality' may look like in a particular subject.

Bonus objective

"Success doesn't mean the absence of failures; it means the attainment of ultimate objectives." Edwin Bliss

Plan one less objective and instead build in a bonus objective, which will be decided upon during the lesson in response to the learners' needs.

AfL is responsive and adaptive to learners needs. Using a medical analogy, if the patient isn't responding then the treatment has to be adapted.

Whilst many advocate that learning objectives should be planned and shared with pupils as part of good practice, inevitably new learning needs, which need greater attention, will transpire during the lesson. Such responsive teaching is at the heart of AfL, as emerging needs are identified and addressed.

The difficulty is that lessons are often rigidly planned and teachers are not inclined to deviate from a lesson plan. One way to overcome this is to build in a 'bonus objective' as part of a teacher's normal planning. The bonus objective isn't an additional objective; it should replace an existing objective and be specifically aimed at responding to an aspect of learning that has emerged in the lesson.

The rationale for this is to refocus the teaching to be responsive rather than rigid, but it also requires rethinking about planning, teaching and learning in order for it to be successful.

Taking it further

In the same way that teachers often share learning objectives with pupils, the bonus objective can also be shared. When sharing the objectives, the bonus objective should be signalled as something that 'we' will decide later in the lesson.

Bonus idea ★

You can involve pupils in deciding what the bonus objective is. It is important that the focus is on the learning and not the activity, but this is an excellent way of responding to learners' needs.

Whiteboard screensaver

"No you don't have to share all your objectives with your pupils at the start of the lesson – likewise you might not want to keep them a secret!"

Displaying your objectives (if you decide to share them) in different ways helps keep the learning focused in the direction it is meant to be travelling.

Teaching tip

Part of good teaching is keeping your approaches fresh, not just for the pupils but also for yourself. It is good to try new ideas without knowing if they will work.

Bonus idea ★

Using scrolling text also seems to work on the screensaver, as the eye is naturally caught by the moving text and you are automatically inclined to start reading.

This is probably the easiest and shortest idea in this book. Whilst in most lessons teachers will share their learning objectives in many ways, a very simple way of reminding pupils throughout the lesson is to type the objectives in to your screensaver at the start of each lesson (assuming that you are using a projector connected to your computer).

This approach has been used in a number of schools and is very effective, because when a screensaver turns on it seems to catch your attention. Intuitively you start reading the text (the learning objectives) and it is a timely reminder for pupils of the main focus of the learning. When the objectives appear, pupils immediately start reading them, which they would be unlikely to repeatedly do if the objectives were presented in a conventional way.

Proxies for learning

"I've never let my school interfere with my education." Mark Twain

Some of the characteristics that we consider good indicators of learning may not indicate learning at all.

It is always a contentious issue when you explain to someone that you can't see learning taking place. This is because there is an assumption that learning will automatically happen just because a teacher is trying to communicate something in a format that will help learning – but this assumption is not true.

The reality is that learning is happening all the time in the classroom and is almost impossible to stop. Unfortunately, the learning taking place may have little to do with what the teacher had hoped to teach. Rachel might be learning that she prefers purple to red, whilst William might be learning that he doesn't like geography. These are hardly what the teacher had planned and are very difficult to prevent.

Many of the norms we think represent good learning indicators are taken as a gauge that successful learning has taken place when the reality is they are poor indicators of learning – but may be good indicators of others factors, such as well-behaved pupils.

The point of highlighting this is that if we want to have really good indicators of effective teaching and learning taking place, we may have to work harder to find such indicators – usually using AfL strategies in an authentic way.

Teaching tip

Research from Durham University has found some poor indicators of learning, including: classroom behaviour is good and under control; students are busy and on task; students are engaged, interested, motivated; the curriculum content is being covered/delivered; the teacher is busy with pupils providing feedback and giving attention; the students seem to know the answers and can reproduce the desired answers to questions.

Pupils as teachers

"If we teach today's students as we taught yesterday's, we rob them of tomorrow." John Dewey

Increasing pupils' autonomy by giving them a role as a 'pupil-teacher' can be used to promote AfL strategies and emphasise learning.

Teaching tip

Teachers work incredibly hard in the classroom, but, although it has become something of a cliché, working smarter is a way forward that many teachers could adopt. Pupils should be working as hard or harder than the teacher, and whilst it is laudable to see teachers helping pupils this often translates into teachers actually doing the work for pupils, which creates the impression of learning when the intended learning isn't really happening.

A natural extension to pupils taking responsibility for their own learning is for them to take responsibility for others' learning. A simple strategy is as follows:

- Prior to a lesson, identify pupils (a group of four or five) to act as teachers.
- Give the pupil-teachers some key instructions about their role and what they need to do. This can be before the lesson, using a teaching assistant to pass on the information or via written instructions.
- Give the pupil-teachers a lanyard or badge to identify them.
- Share the ground rules for pupil-teachers with the whole class. For example, they are there to promote learning – they can't give out detentions or go into the staffroom!
- The pupil-teachers will work in groups asking pre-planned questions (from you), leading on an episode of learning, emphasising the shared criteria, etc.
- Debrief pupil-teachers at the end and use it as a source of feedback – what went well and what could be improved?

The purpose of pupil-teachers is to emphasise pupils' increasing autonomy, but also to shift pupils' perceptions from the teacher as an enforcer of rules to someone primarily concerned with learning – hence the focus on defining the role of the pupil-teacher.

It's all about the right answer – wrong!

"Those who cannot assess cannot teach."

Asking questions is about more than simply trying to elicit the correct answer.

Research in mathematics education suggests that in many lessons, a third of pupils will already know the topic, a third still won't know the topic at the end and only one third will learn what was planned.

Why do teachers ask a question when they (probably) already know the answer?

Perhaps it is to judge pupil understanding and their own effectiveness. This could be misconception, as simply getting the right answer (if there is such a thing) tells you only a small amount about what someone appears to know and how effective the teaching was.

For example, a correct response to a question could be a wild guess, it could be that the pupil has relied on heavy prompts from the teacher or another pupil could have whispered the answer. The correct answer alone may not be sound evidence of teacher effectiveness and pupil understanding.

We sometimes need to recognise that getting the right answer isn't what we are after! Although it may appear counterintuitive, finding out what a pupil doesn't know and using this as a starting point is central to formative and diagnostic teaching and assessment.

Teaching tip

Be aware of the clues you are giving out when asking questions. For example, I have seen a fairly experienced teacher having an apparently successful lesson: pupils were engaged and there were lots of questions being fired around the room with pupils eventually giving the correct response. However, the teacher would best be described as playing charades: he was giving so many clues, in an act of desperation, in order to give the appearance of learning taking place.

Sharing the secret

"It's like knowing the teacher's secret." Pupil definition of AfL

Sharing criteria with pupils requires a particular view of what learning means.

For many years, teaching seemed to involve keeping assessment criteria a secret from learners, as it was the teacher's role to apply the criteria. Sharing the criteria, however, allows the learner to engage in both a summative process (for example, how have I done?) by awarding themselves a grade or a mark and a formative process (for example, how am I doing and what do I need to do to get better?) by identifying how they need to improve. Most importantly, the learner is engaged in a joined up process of reflection and action.

Ultimately, by sharing assessment criteria, teachers are empowering learners by allowing them to navigate their own route through the learning, as well as allowing them into the previously secret garden of knowing how to recognise where they are in their learning and how they need to improve.

Therefore is important to remember:

- The teacher has to makes explicit reference to criteria which should clearly link to the shared learning objectives.
- The criteria has to be in a language that learners understand.
- The learners should have opportunities to engage in self- and peer-assessment.
- A model of how the criteria can be met should be provided for learners.

Ghost children

"I see ghost children!"

It is important to try to engage with all learners, particularly those that might not normally come to your attention.

Ghost children tend to have average ability, average names and average behaviour. They don't set the classroom alight, and often their main ambition is to get through a lesson without being noticed or having their name called out. Then comes that embarrassing moment at parents evening when the teacher realises that they have nothing to discuss except the data they have for the pupil.

An important strategy is to target intervention for all pupils on a regular basis for short, one-to-one, formative discussions. These may be just a few minutes long, but the point it is that they are planned for *all* pupils.

It is unrealistic to do this every lesson, so adopt a strategy of targeting a number of pupils each lesson; all pupils should engaged in a one-to-one discussion at least once every four or five lessons.

Other strategies for engaging the ghost children include:

- Targeted planned questions specifically aimed at those pupils who don't often contribute in lessons.
- Specifically targeting the middle – those pupils who are neither excelling nor struggling.
- Using self- and peer-assessment strategies with all pupils.
- When using group work, ensuring each member is designated with an active role.

Teaching tip

Ensure that the correct emotional environment is established, as there may be additional reasons why a pupil does not wish to participate in a lesson.

Taking it further

Systematically marking on a class list at the start of a year who you are going to see and when across the year, along with accompanying notes, is a simple but effective way of ensuring this activity takes place.

AfL self-assessment checklist

"Intelligence is best defined as knowing what to do when you don't know what to do." Jean Piaget

This self-assessment checklist shows you how AfL can be embedded in your teaching.

- I design lessons with AfL strategies built in.
- Prior to the lesson I identify pupils who I will target for additional support or extension activities, asking questions to, and one-to-one assessment opportunities.
- I share/negotiate/discuss learning with pupils in appropriate ways, developing a shared understanding of what success looks like.
- I build in opportunities and time for acting and reflecting upon previous feedback.
- Feedback is taken from pupils throughout the lesson in different forms.
- Questioning is sophisticated and differentiated. Targeted questions, wait times and Think – Pair – Share (see Idea 7) activities are used frequently.
- Pupil dialogue is encouraged and structured through peer review. The emotional climate and language of feedback are carefully considered for AfL. The feedback sandwich approach is used as appropriate (see Idea 49).
- Assessment is developed through a layered approach, including teacher assessment, self-assessment and peer-assessment.
- Opportunities for metacognition are built into lessons. Pupil motivation is considered.
- AfL is embedded and refined as part of practice through peer review, coaching or lesson study.

Assessment without levels

"Assessment without levels allows a school to emphasise what it values, not what can be measured."

The move to assessment without levels for the national curriculum will prove a challenge for teachers, as well as an opportunity to regain control of assessment practices.

A move has been made to remove national assessment levels from the English education system. This seems radical, but it is no more so than the initial idea of national levels of attainment, first introduced as part of the national curriculum in the late 1980s.

The government will provide guidelines on what represents best practice, but it is up to individual schools to determine how they best assess pupils.

Whilst this presents a challenge, it is also an opportunity for schools to reconsider their approach to assessment. Moving away from national levels allows teachers to shape and value assessment in the way that they wish and to prioritise what they value. It also allows schools and departments to consider:

- What do we value most in learning and how do we capture this?
- What are the best ways to assess pupils and at what stages should we be doing this?
- How do we track pupils' progress?
- How do we get the balance right between summative and formative assessments?
- How do we ensure assessment is reliable and valid?

Teaching tip

DfE Assessment Principle: Schools will be expected to demonstrate (with evidence) their assessment of pupils' progress, to keep parents informed, to enable governors to make judgements about the school's effectiveness, and to inform Ofsted inspections.

Taking it further

A further area for schools to consider is how they communicate what pupils have learned to pupils and parents, and how best to educate both pupils and parents about the changes.

Growth 'mindsets' and AfL

"No matter what your ability is, effort is what ignites that ability and turns it into accomplishment." Carol Dweck

Pupils often feel their position in a hierarchy of learners is fixed due to innate ability rather fluid based upon continued effort.

As a teacher, it is always impressive to see how good pupils are at ranking each other in varying ways (from sporting to academic performance) but always surprising how bad pupils are at locating themselves in any rankings. Typically, those with low self-esteem rank themselves significantly lower than their true position whilst those with an inflated view of themselves rate themselves significantly higher than their actual position.

This is one reason why AfL strategies are so important: they allow pupils to be more accurate in their self-identification of where they are, so that they have a better chance of getting where they want to be.

Pupils' ideas of where they are can also be part of a 'fixed mindset', which Carol Dweck has identified as problematic when pupils think they are fixed in their position because of their innate ability. Pupils with a fixed mindset will often respond to a low assessment by giving up, as opposed to those with a growth mindset, who see it as an opportunity to improve.

As part of AfL it is important to try to instil a growth mindset which:

- encourages persistence
- recognises effort as the route to improvement
- sees failure as valuable learning
- values feedback.

Do I have time for AfL?

"AfL is not asking teachers to work harder but it is definitely expecting pupils to work smarter."

Getting AfL to work with the limited time available will often require a rethink of existing practices.

A genuine question that many teachers ask is 'where does all the time for AfL come from?' It might sound paradoxical, but AfL shouldn't necessarily need more time – it means a better use of existing time. It also adheres to the 'less is more' principle: less but more effective and targeted teacher intervention can be more productive than widespread blanket summative teacher assessment.

For example, most schools give out large amounts of homework and as part of the school culture this will be marked, turned around and given back to pupils in a very short space of time, so that more marking and more homework can be done – a never ending, unquestioned cycle. This can be a hollow, whirlwind process with little time for quality feedback and reflection.

A shift is therefore required in learning, in the school's accountability culture and in parental expectations. School managers and parents have to realise the greater benefits of AfL and understand that it involves a shift to improving the quality of feedback to learners, as well as increasing learner autonomy. This means that the learners have to take on an increased responsibility for managing their own learning so that more time may be spent on planning for learning and ensuring high-level engagement and thinking, rather than trying to catch out who was or wasn't listening when it is already too late.

Teaching tip

Hopefully you have already been thinking that there are lots of great AfL ideas, but you might be worried that you don't have time to implement them. My response is, first, can you afford *not* to implement AfL ideas? And second, AfL is simply good teaching practice, and you shouldn't need to consider whether or not to include it.

From good to outstanding in a discerning way

"A difference between good teaching and outstanding teaching is the effective use of AfL strategies!"

The difference between good and outstanding teaching is often the extent to which AfL strategies are effectively employed.

There are many long discussions and debates to be had about whether or not teachers should be graded for the quality of their teaching in lessons and most recently Ofsted has moved away from grading individual teachers' lessons.

Despite this, there is little debate to be had about whether all teachers should aspire to be 'outstanding' teachers – whatever this actually means. However, in this penultimate idea, I am going to make a pitch that the difference between a 'good teacher' and an 'outstanding teacher' is the extent to which they employ AfL strategies at the right time in the right way.

Any one of the ideas in this book, used at the wrong time in the wrong way, will have little positive impact or, worse still, could have a negative impact. Teachers have to be discerning; they have to know when to use the ideas in this book, when to adapt them, when to persevere with them, when to find out more and when to simply give up on an idea. Teachers are professionals and have to exercise professional judgement about how they teach in order to enhance learning. This means knowing what 'outstanding' teaching and learning looks and feels like, rather than being told how to teach through employing simple rules and step-by-step processes.

Aggregation of marginal gains

"Whilst a wrong assessment made by a teacher may not be life-threatening, a poor diagnosis can stay with a child for a lifetime!"

If you look for improvement in teaching in lots of different areas, collectively they will add up to make you a great teacher.

This book presents 100 ideas, all trying to improve, understand and enhance what happens in a learning environment. Some ideas will sit with the reader easily and others will not but it is only through the relentless pursuit of trying to improve as a professional that you will become a better teacher. This means trying things out, reflecting on what does and doesn't work, and continually finding out more by going deeper in your understanding of your subject and teaching repertoire. Most significantly it means:

- understanding your subject comprehensively
- understanding your pupils in your class in your school
- understanding how best to encourage learning based upon the two previous points.

There are very few quick fixes in the classroom. The British cycling team has a philosophy of improvement though the aggregation of marginal gains, and this is what I recognise in very successful teachers – there is not one major thing that they do well in, but rather it is the aggregation of marginal gains in many different areas that gives them an edge.

Teaching tip

Assessment takes up to a third of a teacher's time, and, in the same way as a doctor avoids getting their diagnosis wrong, teachers also have to be skilled professionals to ensure they make the right decision at the right time.

Taking it further

Teaching is an incredibly complex activity, whilst learning is messy, unpredictable and hard to see. Therefore, teaching is sometimes about getting fewer things wrong than something magical happening. Seeking to improve your strategies in questioning, in feedback, through increased dialogue and challenge will allow the marginal gains to ultimately have significant impact upon your pupils.

References

Assessment Reform Group, (2002) 'Research-based principles to guide classroom practice.'

Bandura, A. (1986), *Social foundations of thought and action: A social cognitive theory.* Englewood Cliffs, NJ: Prentice- Hall, Inc.

Black, P. and Wiliam, D. (2002) 'Feedback is the best nourishment' *Times Educational Supplement.* 4 October 2002.

Brophy, J. (1981), 'Teacher praise: A functional analysis' *Review of Educational Research,* 51: 5–32.

Brown, P. C., Roediger, H. L. and McDaniel, M. A., (2014), *Make it stick: The science of successful learning.* Cambridge: Harvard University Press.

Department for Children, Schools and Families, (2008), 'The assessment for learning strategy.' Nottingham: DCSF Publications.

Department for Education and Employment, (1996) 'Setting Targets to Raise Standards: A Survey of Good Practice.' London: HMSO.

Department of Education and Science and the Welsh Office, (1988), 'National Curriculum Task Group on Assessment and Testing: A Report.'

Dweck, C. (2007), *Mindset: The new psychology of success.* New York: Ballantine books.

Fisher, R. (1998), *Teaching Thinking.* London: Cassell.

Gibbs, G and Simpson, C. (2004), 'Conditions under which assessment supports students' learning' *Learning and Teaching in Higher Education.* 1, 3–31.

Hattie, J. and Timperley, H. (2007), 'The power of feedback' *Review of Educational Research.* 77, 81–112.

Haney, W. (1991), 'We must take care: Fitting assessments to functions' in V.Perrone (ed.), *Expanding Student Assessment.* Alexandria: VA: Association for Supervision and Curriculum Development.

James, M., Black, P., Carmichael, P., Drummond, M.J., Fox, A., MacBeath, J., McCormick, R., Pedder, D., Procter, R., Swaffield, S., Swann, J. & Wiliam, D. (2007) *Improving Learning How to Learn: classrooms, schools and networks.* London: Routledge.

MacBeath, J., (2010), 'Leadership for learning: concepts, principles and practice' *Leadership for Learning, The Cambridge Network.* Cambridge: LFL.

Ofsted, (2015), *The school inspection handbook*. London: HMSO.

Ofsted, (1996), 'Subjects and standards: Issues for school development arising from OFSTED inspection findings 1994–5. Key Stages 3 & 4 and post-16.' London: HMSO.

Perrenoud, P. (1991), 'Towards a pragmatic approach to formative evaluation' in *Assessment of pupil's achievements: Motivation and school success*, ed. P. Weston Amsterdam, Swets and Zeitlinger.

Perrenoud, P. (1998), 'From formative evaluation to a controlled regulation of learning processes: Towards a wider conceptual field', *Assessment in education: Principles, policy and practice.* 5, 85–102.

Popham. W. James, (2008), *Transformative assessment.* Alexandria: ASCD.

Sadler, D. R. (1989) 'Formative assessment and the design of instructional systems' *Instructional Science.* 18 (2),

Warnock, H. M. (1978), 'The Warnock Report: Special Educational Needs.' London: HMSO.